Tradition in Crisis

Sept- 10

To Phyllis

For friendship in work and faith.

Peter

Tradition in Crisis

The Case for Centric Protestants

Peter Schmiechen

WIPF & STOCK · Eugene, Oregon

TRADITION IN CRISIS
The Case for Centric Protestants

Wipf & Stock
An Imprint of Wipf and Stock Publishers
199 W. 8th Ave., Suite 3
Eugene, OR 97401

www.wipfandstock.com

PAPERBACK ISBN: 978-1-6667-4649-5
HARDCOVER ISBN: 978-1-6667-4650-1
EBOOK ISBN: 978-1-6667-4651-8

08/04/22

To Jan

Contents

Preface

THERE IS SOMETHING AT the heart of the Protestant tradition which makes it distinctive. In my life time it has proven to be a necessary voice in American religion. How it could decline is something of a contradiction, which needs to be explored. But can it be revived? Only if it claims its central message.

For over sixty years I have engaged in prayer, study, conversation, and work on these issues: the heart of the tradition, the crisis, and prospects for revival. I was never able to isolate only one thing since they are so tied together. It has been my good fortune to work on these issues in different settings. First there was the graduate school experience, where christological issues came to the fore, set against the background of the modern age. Then there was teaching at Elmhurst College, where I was required to consider the meaning of faith and its relation to the world, as represented by at least twenty other disciplines. Then came years of working with faculty and pastors at Lancaster Seminary. With assistance from the Lilly Endowment in the 1990s we were able to explore ways renewal might take place by an openness to the gospel. Rev. Claude Dencler, pastor and staff colleague at Lancaster Seminary, was an important part of this process and I am grateful for his leadership. Another colleague was Dr. Nathan Baxter, a graduate of Lancaster Seminary, who became Dean of the Seminary. An Episcopal priest, Dr. Baxter later became Episcopal Bishop of the Diocese of Central Pennsylvania. He has been a long-time friend and source of inspiration.

Preface

In the past twenty years I have written on atonement theory, the church, and the Lord's Supper. In each of these studies, attention was directed at a central issue in theology, but always in the context of the search for what form the gospel might take in the context of Protestantism in America. Over these years I have had several conversation partners who have consistently inspired and have given support: Dr. Lee C. Barrett, Lancaster Seminary, Dr. Linden DeBie, Reformed Church in America, and Dr. William B. Evans, of Erskine College. In recent years it has been a source of encouragement to be in conversation with H. Paul Santmire, who I first met at Harvard in 1962. He has continually addressed the ecological crisis as a theological issue, requiring changes in our faith and practice. Rev. Thomas Lush, a UCC pastor, has for years challenged many with the need to find new forms for faith and practice in the face of the church crisis. His concerns for the care of people and the faithful confession of the gospel have inspired me to pursue this project. Rev. James Weaver, a Presbyterian pastor, has also been a helpful commentator as this project took form. Rev. William Worley, Conference Minister, Pennsylvania South East Conference of the United Church of Christ has also provided valuable insight as the project came to conclusion. For their interest and encouragement I am grateful.

I also wish to thank several staff members at Wipf and Stock for their encouragement and assistance in bringing this project to publication: Rodney Clapp, Editor, Matt Wimer, Managing Editor, and Caleb Kormann, Copyeditor.

Introduction

Purpose

THIS IS AN ESSAY about naming and claiming the essence of centric Protestantism. It is a tradition generated by the Reformers' affirmation of grace and the reform of the medieval Mass and the life of the church. In the face of the modern age it reformulated Christian faith in terms of the centrality of Christ, rather than appeals to an absolute doctrine or Bible. In the twentieth century it was renewed by a series of revolutions in theology and biblical studies. It broke with the individualism and optimism of the American liberal tradition and resisted attempts to define religion in terms of the authority of the church, doctrine, or an infallible Bible. Given two world wars, genocide in Europe and racism in America, it insisted that issues of justice and peace must be addressed. It is an heir to the Reformation, not in spite of all these reactions and reforms, but because of them. For this reason it represents a quite distinct and necessary voice in American religion.[1]

The structure of the essay follows the key moments in the tradition's faith and practice: (1) the grace of God in Jesus Christ; (2) grace and community; (3) sin and grace; (4) the principle of authority; (5) worship and the vital center.

One may not, however, describe the tradition in an ideal way without recognizing—and if possible, coming to terms with—the crisis which

1. For a definition and discussion of the term *centric Protestants*, see the last four pages of this introduction.

1

began in the 1960s and extends to the present day. The obvious form of the crisis has to do with loss in numbers, congregations, and dollars. But the crisis also involves the emergence of adversarial and—at times—hostile relations between the tradition and the culture as well as conservative Protestants. Churches discovered that the culture and/or government could be far more antithetical to Christian faith than previously assumed. Likewise, the struggles with other Protestants were so serious that they came to be called a "culture war." But there were also contradictions in the tradition itself which contributed to the crisis. Faith itself could be compromised and subverted in a variety of ways. To put it simply, centric Protestants found themselves in a culture opposed to its basic values, quarrelling with conservative Protestants, and having to deal with their own problems of faith and practice.

Crisis as Loss

The initial symptom of the crisis is an overwhelming sense of loss as church leaders witnessed an end of an era. It begins with decline in membership and dollars, then staff changes, perhaps a reduction to part time pastors and in some cases dissolving congregations. Consider some of the data: The United Methodists have lost roughly 40 percent between 1960 and 2020, if you combine Methodist and Evangelical United Brethren membership before their merger.[2] The United Church of Christ has lost about 57 percent since 1970.[3] The Episcopal Church lost roughly 1.6 million members between the 1960's and 2018.[4] The PCUSA lost 61 percent of members from 1983 to 2020.[5] In 1988 the ELCA listed 5.1 million members, a number reduced to 3.1 million in 2020. Since 2009 it lost half a million members and seven hundred congregations, largely related to the decision regarding human sexuality.[6] If you are wondering how conservatives have fared, the Missouri Lutherans lost 26 percent of members between 1970 and 2015, while the Southern Baptist Convention grew from 10.7 million members in 1965 to 16.6 million in 2006, but lost 15 percent since 2006.[7] While the

2. "United Methodist Church: Membership Trends," *Wikipedia*.

3. "United Church of Christ: Membership," *Wikipedia*.

4. Egan Millard, "Parochial Reports," *Episcopal News Service*.

5. "Presbyterian Church–USA: Demographics," *Wikipedia*.

6. "Evangelical Lutheran Church in America: Demographics," *Wikipedia*.

7. For Missouri Lutherans, cf. "Lutheran Church-Missouri Synod," *Wikipedia*; for

ELCA figures may relate to controversial social decisions, interpretations of UCC losses point in a different direction: data there suggests that a major source of decline was the loss of young people after confirmation.[8] This would explain the significant increase in losses since 2000. For the UCC from 1965–2000 the rates of decline were between 3.02–8.3 percent, whereas since 2000 the rates increased to 9.8–13.9 percent.[9]

Loss of members and dollars shows up in three important areas: First, a decline in developmental programs for support of congregations and pastors. This area of church life was also affected by the amount of time regional officials gave to pastors in personal crisis, churches in conflict, budget problems and placement for low membership congregations. For example, in the UCC, there was little time for formative or developmental programs. In effect, regional staff time was preoccupied with crisis management.

Second, there were major changes in the demographics of students preparing for ministry. Beginning with the 1970s, four changes occurred:

a. a decline in students between 22–25, especially white males;

b. an increase in female students;

c. an increase in average age;

d. a general decline in total number, which for many seminaries reached crisis proportions since 2000.

Taken together this meant an increase in commuting students in contrast to resident students, as well as an increase in the denominational mix of students at centric Protestant seminaries. There is much to celebrate regarding the increase in female students, average age, and denominational mix. But a decline in total numbers means less tuition for seminaries which are tuition dependent. A general decline in church members also means less aid for students and a decline in contributions in support of seminaries. One should also add that when seminaries start reducing faculty and programs, it affects churches as well as students. Many seminaries had added to their mission specific programs to assist pastors and congregations. When seminaries themselves faced shortfalls, these programs suffered.

The third area affected by the general church crisis was the support of full time pastors. Loss of members and dollars affected pastoral

Southern Baptists, cf. "Southern Baptists," *Wikipedia*.

8. Cf. Roof and McKinney, *American Mainline Religion*, 11–39.

9. "United Church of Christ: Membership," *Wikipedia*.

compensation and reduced the number of congregations able to support a full time pastor. This created a complicated debate over whether we had too many or too few pastors. One can imagine the impact of such a debate on those considering seminary. What we have then, is a church crisis at every level of the organization, with many of the negative numbers getting worse since 2000.

Crisis as a New Relation to Culture

One thing emerging from the crisis is a new awareness of the complicated relation between centric Protestant churches and the American tradition. On the one hand Protestants warmly embraced the notion that America is a nation founded on a set of values, such as liberty, equality, and justice. On the other hand, there have always been contradictions regarding these values, the most obvious one being the existence of slavery, leading to the Civil War. Some of these tensions have always been there, overshadowed by the positive relations between Protestants and the culture. What has happened during the past six decades is the greater awareness by centric Protestants that aspects of the culture are antithetical to Christian faith. Consider several examples.

First, in the new political order religion was defined as a right of the individual, freed from kings, tradition, and bishops. In turn, religious groups came to be seen as voluntary associations of like-minded people. Moreover, churches came to be seen as functional entities existing to do what individuals could not do, but not endowed with special value. This basic framework undercuts the idea of the church in several ways: (a) it defines things in terms of the individualism dominant in American society. One can be religious and not go to church; one can even separate Jesus from the church. (b) It bases the unity of the church on our agreement. Since such like-mindedness is sorely tested by controversial doctrinal and social issues, it soon became clear that churches divide time and again in search of the goal of singlemindedness. In such a world, the idea that we are bound together by Christ in spite of differences is lost. (c) The functional view of the church, i.e., it is important only when I need it, undercuts the Christian affirmation that community is an essential form of human existence. Fast forward to the decades of the current crisis and we find churches speaking the language of American individualism. Religion is all about God and me;

4

there can be no unity unless we agree; the church really isn't essential to the individual's religious journey.[10]

Second, while the founders proposed a new nation based on freedom and equality, they perpetuated many of the repressive values which marked the old colonial order of English monarchs. For example, that rulers have the right to claim new land from indigenous peoples, the right to enslave peoples to create cheap labor, and to perpetuate the hierarchy of men over women. In the ongoing debate over race, the institution of slavery has rightly been called America's original sin. Like that original sin envisioned in Christian doctrine, it led to terrifying consequences: the forcible removal of Africans to America and centuries of slavery, leading ultimately to the Civil War. Nor has the relation of white to black been resolved. In fact, in the political environment of 2021 the subject is so controversial it is difficult—and in some places illegal—to speak of racial inequalities still perpetuated by the social order. The contradictions of our culture are not limited to those involving slavery. There is also the matter of genocidal practices toward indigenous peoples, and the exclusion of other minorities of color. Moreover, it has taken several centuries to affirm the equality of women. When churches buy into these limitations on freedom and equality, the unity in Christ is usually compromised.

Third, the question may be asked whether we have ever set aside the colonial mindset. Colonies are created by a homeland to allow for expansion and production of resources and goods. This colonial mindset produced two consequences: on the one hand, land exists to be acquired, used and exploited. The environmental crisis reveals how alienated we are from nature; we do not see ourselves a part of nature but see it as an object for our use. On the other hand, we continue to think as colonists, namely, that our purpose is to produce more and consume more. To be sure, we do not send goods back to England as the seat of empire, but we do expect citizens to use more and more of everything and we confer value upon people in terms of what they have acquired. Colonialism has thus been transformed into a material culture where more is always better. But this requires a long list of inequalities and the exploitation of the environment. Are Christians willing to support this?

---

10. For an extensive analysis of these ideas, cf. Bellah et al., *Good Society* and Bellah, et. al., *Habits of the Heart.*

Crisis as Culture Wars

In the post-WWII era, mainline Protestants acknowledged that we were no longer a Protestant nation and welcomed a new pluralism of Protestant, Catholic, and Jew. Of course it had been that way for centuries, though even in the 1950s some refused to admit it. No one dreamed of including Muslims or Buddhists, or that there would come a time when a significant portion of the population would not identify itself with organized religion. The other thing about this consensus was that little attention was paid to conservative Protestants. All this soon changed as one crisis after another rocked the U.S., creating a divide between liberals and conservatives in politics and religion. Each stage of the crisis introduced new elements, which intensified the opposition between groups, prompting James D. Hunter to describe it as a "culture war:" multiple issues dividing people over time with cumulative negative results.[11] This culture war has extended to the present time, too often manipulated by political parties to generate fear or anger, in the hope of election victories. For churches, it meant a new way of dividing centric and conservative Protestants, along with other historic religious and theological differences. But it also created divisions within centric Protestant churches, since they found themselves internally divided on every issue. What developed by the 1970s was a new alignment of centric Protestants versus conservative Protestants, viewing each other across a field of battle where social-political issues were dominant. Most important, what began in the 1960s became the context for the significant decline of centric Protestants. What caused the decline is still under debate, since other things were happening in the culture affecting religious affiliation. What is of special interest for this study is how centric Protestants reacted to the cultural crises as well as the decades of decline.

Beginning in 1963, three issues were catalysts for change:

The first was the civil rights movement that emerged in a variety of groups, mobilizing thousands of people to protest racial inequality in America. The most well-known was that of Martin Luther King, Jr., who developed a non-violent form of social and political action to bring about changes in laws and social structures. If you like symbols, think of King's "Letter From Birmingham City Jail."[12]

---

11. Cf. Hunter, *Culture Wars: The Struggle to Define America*, 31–51, 106–32.
12. King, Jr., "Letter from Birmingham City Jail."

The second was the Vietnam War, following a decade after the Korean War, both part of America's response to aggression by the Soviet Union. Both wars must also be placed in the context of WWII, where America emerged victorious from a horrifying war in Europe and the Pacific, vowing to create a new world order. What started as minor assistance to a pro-western government in Vietnam grew into a major war, with the government convinced that its superior military strength and technology would result in victory. As a symbol of this crisis, think of David Halberstam's book, *The Best and the Brightest.*[13]

The third was Watergate, extending from the break in on June 17, 1962 to Nixon's resignation, August 7, 1974. In this case, a president of a party claiming bedrock values sought to conceal an attempt to gain leverage in a coming election. As a symbol of this crisis, think of *All the President's Men*, by Carl Bernstein and Robert Woodward.[14]

Why recall these three crises? Each revealed a fundamental problem regarding the law, human suffering and abuse of trust. Even more frightening, there was no great majority agreement on any issue. In the case of King's letter, we find an appeal to the Constitution and essentials of Christian faith, only to have Christians divide, in both south and north. In the case of the war, Halberstam's book laid bare how one of the greatest tragedies in American history could be planned, sanctioned and defended for years by the best and brightest, energized by the victory in WWII and the optimism of a new Democratic administration. Then lay alongside that the abuse of power in Watergate by a Republican administration, convinced that they could break the law and then lie to the American people. The point is that the culture war exposed two quite different responses to the crises over race, the war and corruption in government. Each case involved a crisis of trust: would government and the society fulfill the promise of the American dream? If the mistrust and rage were initially directed at the government, they soon were directed at other institutions allied with the government, i.e. churches, universities, and corporations.

The emergence of mistrust as a dominant framework for identity relates to two major developments: one is that in the ensuing decades, young people will opt out of organized religion and the percentage of unaffiliated as a category for adults will increase from 8 percent in 1990 to 22.8

---

13. Halberstam, *Best and the Brightest.*
14. Bernstein and Woodward, *All the President's Men.*

percent in 2014.[15] A striking example of such disaffiliation came when I was teaching college students in the early 70s. When I asked why they did not identify themselves as Christians, their answer was that the people who used Christian language were the ones supporting the war, segregation, and opposition to women's rights. The other development is the rise of mistrust of adults toward major institutions in American society (i.e., government, universities, health systems, national churches, public education and major corporations). This became a major theme in interpretations of the 2016 election and continues to be a factor in the politics of anger and grievance.

Were We Prepared for the Crisis?

The simple answer is no. Centric Protestants were not prepared to find themselves opposing the culture over individualism, equal rights, and rampant materialism. Nor were they prepared to engage conservative Protestants in a running cultural war for sixty years. In faith and practice there were contradictions, gaps and compromises. It is important to acknowledge this, not simply to re-litigate the past sixty years, but to recognize how the tradition itself contributed to the crisis. For a tradition in crisis, there must be an honest appraisal of the way we have come. In that spirit, consider these factors which affected the tradition's response to the crises.

Private and Public Faith

In spite of the movement by neo-orthodox leaders to move toward a more critical engagement with the world, centric Protestants were quite comfortable with confining religion to the individual life and the life of congregations. This resulted in what one might call a disconnect of ethics from religion. Time and time again, members and congregations could not understand how the emerging social issues related to faith in Jesus Christ. Recall how priests and nuns, ministers and rabbis marching for racial justice would be asked: "Why are you doing this?" Likewise, the emergence of movements for the rights of women, indigenous people and LGBT were too often met with bewilderment and opposition. It was as if the *older brother* had taken center stage. The *older brother* refers to that third character in the parable of the prodigal son, who believes the world should be ordered

15. "Irreligion in the United States: Demographics," *Wikipedia*.

by rules, that the good should be rewarded and the bad punished, and that achievement is what counts. You know the older brother is present when discussions about helping the poor or expanding health care bring up the issue of whether they *deserve* such benefits. What stood out in endless debates over aid or access to the benefits of a free society was the cold-hearted refusal, based on a lack of compassion. This was shocking because in Protestant piety, grace generates gratitude, which is the engine driving works of love and compassion. Compassion is like the canary in the coal mine: where there is no compassion one fears that there is an absence of gratitude, which in turn means a misunderstanding regarding grace. The question then is: were we unable to respond in more positive ways because we had settled into a view of religion restricted to individual life, which in effect allows for a loss of compassion?

Love and Power

Reinhold Niebuhr had made a persuasive case that while love is the highest moral value, social justice could only be achieved by the use of coercive power, with non-violent coercion being the preferred strategy.[16] While Niebuhr could hold these two together—most churches could not, which meant that the relation of love and power was basically unresolved. Given the priority of sacrificial love, can one as a Christian engage in coercive force, be it non-violent or violent? Martin Luther King, Jr.'s movement was a breakthrough because it declared that Christians as Christians could engage in non-violent coercion in the cause of equality. The problem was that most Protestants did not know what to make of it, as evidence by the letter from religious leaders which produced his "Letter from Birmingham City Jail" stating his case.[17] In effect, Protestants of all persuasions were not prepared for black people, women, or environmentalists protesting in the name of equality and justice. The result was continuous debate over strategy which proved contentious and divisive.

16. Cf. Reinhold Niebuhr, *Moral Man and Immoral Society*.
17. King, Jr. "Letter."

Bible Battles

Any struggle in the name of freedom or equality must ground its claim in something authoritative. One of the reasons centric Protestants were not prepared for the crises was that they were not prepared for a fight over the Bible. Let me explain: When Luther wanted to protest certain practices, resistance to change came from those appealing to tradition and church authority. While he could have appealed to Augustine and other traditions, this would have meant a battle between church traditions, ultimately decided by papal authority. So instead he appealed to Scripture, claiming it to be a higher authority. Thus began the long and noble tradition of Protestants claiming *sola scriptura*. It is a great strategy when arguing against tradition and church authority. But does it work when both sides appeal to Scripture? What does one do when one side can quote Scripture to protect the status quo of slavery and segregation or the subordination of women? Centric Protestants countered by arguing that *sola scriptura* did not mean the absolute authority of every verse of the Bible but that the Bible should be read from a christological point of view, i.e., the central message of the redemption of Jesus Christ. The problem was that this had not been communicated effectively to members. Perhaps they did get the point that Genesis 1–2 are not to be taken as a literal or scientific account of creation, but it was not at all clear how to interpret the Bible on the social issues of the times such as war, civil rights, women's rights, homosexuality, and abortion. After all, didn't the reading of Scripture on Sunday morning conclude with the words, "the Word of the Lord." As a result, centric Protestants found themselves in a difficult position: they wanted to appeal to the Bible but many of their own people did not understand how they were doing this; the other side charged them with a selective reading of the Bible. When they denied this they also discovered that a heated debate is not the time to introduce the general subject of how we read the Bible. We had not prepared congregations for a fight over the Bible.

The Collapse of Evangelism

One of the strange things during a sixty-year period of decline was the inability of centric Protestants to generate programs of evangelism. They were either reluctant or unwilling to engage the church and the culture with the drama of sin and salvation. It was evident that they were uncomfortable with the word evangelism. For some it suggested the techniques of revivalism while others saw it as becoming snared in the demand for numbers to serve the interests of institutions. Some even defined mission as something completely outside the church. At times evangelism was equated with spiritual growth and discipleship, without much connection to membership. Two examples illustrate this paralysis.

The first was the inability to make the transition from *communities of belonging* to *communities of believing*. Let me explain. Most of us grew up in a community of belonging, surrounded by family and friends. Such communities operated on loyalty and received support from public schools, higher education, and the general culture. Beginning in the 60s, however, all communities of loyalty suffered damage due to personal infidelities, unjust practices toward women and minorities, and complicity in dishonest policies. Corporations, governments, educational institutions, and yes, religious organizations proved to be fallible by means of betrayals of trust. In such a situation, appeals to loyalty did not work, since trust had been broken. In churches, few people walked in the doors because of the traditional appeal of religion and, as studies have shown, there was a significant decline in children attending church after confirmation.[18] People asked a new set of questions which came to mark a community of believing: why join, why give, why serve, why participate? This caught pastors and older generations off guard, since our children were supposed to know the answers to such questions. We were organized as communities of belonging based on *loyalty*, but unprepared for answering questions based on *persuasion*. In fairness, pastors were unprepared for this situation, since they had been largely educated to minister to the community of belonging. Pastors faithfully called on the sick and the grieving, and showed up every Sunday, but were not ready for cold calls or impertinent questions. It was quite threatening to be asked to make the case for Christian faith in a hostile world and have to deal with rejection. Denominations at the national and regional levels, as well as seminaries, were slow to respond to preparing pastors for a community of believing based on persuasion. This inability at the congregational level to shift into persuasion reflects the general collapse of evangelism. It was as if we assumed people would naturally join churches, or that congregations were self-perpetuating.

The second example is how our efforts to lift up the wonders of grace ended up disconnecting grace from the church. In a world of so much

18. Cf. Roof and McKinney, 11–39.

legalism and self-righteousness, the gospel was so often reduced to making God's love depend on our achievement and compliance with rules and doctrinal demands. To counter such legalism, centric Protestants countered with the proclamation of unconditional love. For those excluded and/or living in shame, such a message may well be good news. But here's the catch: the declaration of God's love has been disconnected from the call to participate in the community of faith and service. In effect, religion has been reduced to the individual's relation with God, defined by unconditional love. All sense of the church as the people of God on earth, or any sense of eschatological vision for the world has been dropped. If one has heard this message, does one need to hear it again? Without reference to cross and resurrection, the message becomes one of cheap grace.

Mixed Signals on Worship

If one asks, "What is happening in worship?" Roman Catholics give a clear answer: Christ is present in bread and wine, offered to God for our salvation. This exchange assures the forgiveness of sins and our union with Christ. Conservative Protestants will also give a clear answer: the message is proclaimed and this is the time for you to make a decision for Christ. Centric Protestants, however, will give quite different answers and in this way, mixed signals are given.

With respect to the service of the Word, the liberal wing will see it as a gathering to remember the love of God and recommit to service. The majority see it as a sermon-centered service, where gathering, prayers, hymns and Scripture lead up to the sermon, followed by a hymn and benediction. If the sermon is the center, then we must ask how it points to the drama of sin and salvation, to confronting the idols of this world, or to the presence of Christ among us with the celebration of his gifts. Or has the sermon, and worship itself, become so independent on our action that a sense of responding to the presence of Christ has been lost? In such situations the pastor must bear the burden of filling the void, which is an intolerable burden. Something is amiss if the sermon only offers comments on a few verses of Scripture, moral admonitions, or dramatic stories. The same may be said if the only thing happening is the expectation to re-commit to service, when all the while we are unsure why we should do that or how we can.

It is no wonder that centric Protestants have been urged to borrow the practices of others. Some see the answer as being more spiritual, with the use of Roman Catholic spirituality, as if there was no spiritual life in our own tradition. Then others suggest that weekly Eucharist will fill the void. By contrast we have been urged to be more informal, depend less on symbols and set liturgies, adopt seeker services, and sing new music. Such conflicting answers suggest we need clarity as to what is happening.

The appeal to the Lord's Supper to fill the void can also send mixed signals. Luther rejected transubstantiation but, most importantly, the idea that the bread and wine are offered by us with Christ's offering to God to assure salvation. Instead, the Supper was God's gracious act toward us, with Christ fully present in and with the bread and wine. But while Luther rejected the medieval framework, somehow that framework continued to be used among Protestants along with a theology of grace, creating an inevitable contradiction. In the 1950s, Protestants still used the medieval framework where the emphasis was on preparation, sin, repentance, offerings to God and pleas for mercy on behalf of individual sinners. The reliance on a theology of penal substitution, where Christ dies as a sacrifice to appease God in the face of the demands of the law only reenforced the old framework. Since the 1950s every centric Protestant denomination has made one or more changes to the liturgy.[19] These changes have either removed references to penal substitution or revised the language in the attempt to celebrate grace. But there is still much work to be done: the old framework of repentance, pleading for mercy and forgiveness of sins, is still there in most services. Likewise, the language of sacrifice still portrays the Supper as something we offer or bring to God, not God's action toward us. The service still has an individualistic focus: it is all about individuals receiving forgiveness rather than a communal celebration. Finally, most liturgies give little attention to an eschatological vision or the kingdom of God. As a result, there is no time given to celebrating as a community our new life in Christ. We are still pleading for mercy up to the point of receiving the bread and wine. Until we set aside time for a celebration of the community in the context of the coming of the kingdom, there will continue to be an absence of joy. As it stands, we have a very mixed message about what is happening: is it a service of penance and forgiveness or an eschatological celebration of new life in Christ? In effect, the reform of the Lord's Supper is unfinished and the service of the table loses its communal nature and its evangelical center.

---

19. Cf. my discussion of changes in the liturgy among centric Protestants in *Gift and Promise*, Chapter 3.

What we need, then, is to reclaim the tradition. That means beginning with grace and community, followed by affirmations of sin and grace, authority, and worship as celebration of Christ's presence. We need clarity about the message and a new will to proclaim it because the tradition finds itself in quite a different culture than half a century ago. For one thing, it stands more against the culture than as a partner. It also needs clarity in order to differentiate its message from competing religious groups as well as the popular religious self-help programs. The individualism and anti-institutionalism of the society require a major revision in the way we care for the church and persuade both our children and those outside the church to participate in the Christian life. We have learned that the church is not self-perpetuating but depends on proclaiming the new life Christ brings. These are the things which give hope for renewal of the church, where being and doing, worship and service will be bound together by the new life Christ brings. In a world where religion is popular but the church is not, we must turn again to the church's only treasure, namely, Jesus Christ.

Definitions

An explanation is needed regarding the meaning of the words *centric Protestants* as a title for the tradition discussed in this essay. Since the word "Protestant" can cover such a wide range of churches, some modifier is needed, especially since some see the word as referring to all Christians who are not Roman Catholics or Orthodox. But which labels are helpful? The common labels used to differentiate Protestants are not always adequate and are complicated by exceptions. For example, while the liberal-conservative polarity is useful, it can be confusing. There are liberals and conservatives in general, but also liberals and conservatives within each denomination. Some conservative members of the ELCA might appear quite liberal compared to the Lutheran Church—Missouri Synod. Likewise, the groups described in this essay are usually called liberal, even though they repudiated the rationalism and optimism of both political and religious liberalism. Denominational labels may give some directional signals regarding historical origin, but are not always accurate in naming all those that would identify with the themes extolled in this essay. Every Protestant denomination has within it liberals and conservatives, some so opposed to the standard denominational profile that they constitute a faction at war with the majority or are prone to leave. The twentieth-century theological revolutions tended to mute the strict differences between mainline Protestant groups. This emphasis on unifying factors was accelerated by the enrollment of students in seminaries of other denominations, as well as the mix of faculty at each seminary. It is no secret that the most intense battles may be within denominations rather than between them. It is also worth noting that individuals stay with churches for all sorts of reasons besides doctrinal, be it solidarity with family and friends, music, a specific pastor/preacher, or aesthetic reasons. Some Roman Catholics have lost respect for the hierarchy but still value the liturgy with its symbols and music.

Given the complexity of the issue, two methods will be used to define centric Protestants. The first focuses on the central message of Luther and Calvin, namely, the Word of promise in Jesus Christ, understood as grace. This involved the priority of Scripture over against tradition and church, the rejection of the medieval Mass and the reform of the church. This means that centric Protestants are those who claim continuity with the Reformers on these issues.

The second method is historical and follows the way centric Protestants affirmed, adapted, and expanded the basic message over five centuries. Viewed from this perspective, centric Protestants are those claiming three reformations:

1. They celebrate the essential message of the sixteenth-century Reformation, namely the Word of promise in Jesus Christ, understood as grace.

2. They are open to the issues raised by the Enlightenment. This involved responses to quite different challenges. First, the new science proposed a new worldview quite different from the biblical cosmology. Second, critical philosophy denied the proofs for the existence of God, in effect undercutting a rational defense for religion apart from religious faith. Third, the attempt to base faith on the inerrancy of Scripture was questioned repeatedly in terms of historical accuracy, alternate theories of authorship and inconsistencies between texts. Fourth, the Enlightenment demonstrated confidence in reason to reorder society without reliance on tradition, monarchy and church.

While Protestants responded in varied ways to all of these issues, centric Protestants discovered that the christological foundation for faith proved to be decisive in reconstructing theology in light of the new science and the absence of rational proofs. Most important, the christological focus meant an openness to historical-critical study because the priority was Jesus Christ, not an inerrant Bible. What emerged was the new sense that centric Protestants were between two groups: on the left were those allied with the liberal rationalism of Locke and Kant, which gave primacy to individual freedom and too easily reduced religion to ethics and rational ideas. On the right were those more defensive regarding the modern world, favoring instead orthodox doctrine, an inerrant Bible and the social status quo.

3. The third reformation involved the theological and biblical revolutions of the twentieth century, in the context of two world wars, racism in America and genocide against Jews in Europe. This meant a rejection of liberal rationalism and optimism as well as a return to the Reformation themes of sin and grace, Trinity and incarnation, and the church as a community of witnesses for justice and peace. By the second half of the century, liberation theology emerged as a further reform. These reforms in theology and biblical study changed faith and practice in many ways: a more positive view of Judaism and Hebrew Scriptures; an ecumenical vision seen in mergers of denominations, new relations with black churches, sharing of church life and theological education, and a commitment to justice and peace.

The conjunction of the two approaches is decisive. In the first there is the attempt to define a tradition by the central motifs of the sixteenth-century Reformation. Anyone who claims the name "Protestant" must decide whether they claim anything from that reform. But that is not all which defines us because we no longer live in the sixteenth century. In five hundred years the world has changed and the church must choose what is the appropriate and most faithful response to these changes. Luther and Calvin did not have to deal with the modern worldview, Enlightenment critical thinking, or the reforms of the twentieth century. The question then becomes: Is the priority of the Word of promise in Jesus Christ, understood as grace, able to inspire faith in such different and terrifying times? This essay affirms that centric Protestants are those who claim this christological starting point for faith and practice.

Such an approach makes clear why centric Protestants are not defined simply by denominational labels or the qualifiers of liberal and conservative, but the choices made in critical times. It also suggests that the reality of centric Protestantism may include far more believers from other denominations than one might imagine. How these choices differentiate centrist Protestants from others will be pursued in the following chapters. Along the way it will also be argued that this tradition is a distinct and necessary voice in American religion today. One can make this claim without implying that centric Protestants are the only Protestants or the only Christians. Like the definition of centric Protestants, this claim is also now open for discussion and debate.

If there are difficulties in defining centric Protestants, it is just as difficult to define those groups to the right. It has already been noted that the word conservative is used in a variety of ways, since many among the center group are *conservative* or right of center. Likewise, many among denominations that once were deemed very conservative have moved closer to the center without changing denominational labels. Context gives the word quite different meanings. The word "evangelical" does not appear as a solution since it is too general and covers up the distinctions between moderate and extreme positions. In spite of these difficulties, the term conservative appears to be preferable, since "right wing" has such strong political connotations. Not all conservative Protestants have accepted the current union of religious and political beliefs. Here is a working definition of conservative Protestants, involving two parts.

The first is to recognize that there are Protestants who do not identify as either liberal or centric Protestants. Four groups of different origin and theology come to mind, with major qualifications:

1. **Orthodox Lutheran and Reformed Confessionalism,** which prefers to speak in terms of absolute doctrine or an absolute Bible.

2. **Anabaptists,** though some would not be conservative on matters of peace and even theology.

3. **Pentecostals and Charismatics,** whether independent or within other denominations.

4. **Fundamentalists:** those adhering to specific doctrines or some form of biblical inerrancy.

The second distinction involves superimposing on the four groups the distinction between *moderate* and *extreme/militant,* with respect to theology and political involvements. This would allow us to deal with the fact that all four groups differ among themselves and often object to being identified with moderate or extreme positions.

I

Where It All Began

MY YEARS IN GRADUATE school from 1959–69 changed my life. Of course there was the rigor and the stress, the many ways my world was shattered and put back together, and economic hardship. What is relevant for this discussion was the sense that we were living on the brink of radical changes. We had been, in effect, schooled in the ways of modern theology which involved radical engagement with critical thought, closing the doors forever on certain kinds of religiosity. At the same time it opening the way to a new perspective on religion. A large number of writers became for us explorers into an unknown world, where the old was shaken as if by earthquakes and the new appeared in strange ways from ancient as well as contemporary texts. These figures were crucial in rescuing us from despair and agnosticism. The form and substance of the theology emerging was not printed in the sixteenth century, but it was a revised form of Protestant piety.

But just when we were ready to celebrate the transition to a new world, it began to fall apart. Instead of thinking we might spend the rest of our lives writing footnotes on Reinhold Niebuhr, H. Richard Niebuhr, Paul Tillich, Karl Barth, or a dozen other scholars, we suddenly found ourselves not knowing how to do theology. What we had learned, what had become the basis for hope, did not seem to relate to the challenges of the civil rights and anti-war movements. Here was a new methodology: listening to those excluded from mainstream society, reacting to government appraisals of a war, and participating in active resistance. Thus we entered and lived through a half-century of theological endeavors where one revolt after another ushered in a time of radical diversity and pluralism. Theological movements came and went, sometimes flashing like meteors across the night sky. Sometimes there appeared to be peace treaties between old adversaries, at other times things fell apart along the lines of old rivalries and/or the divisions of nature, be it gender, race, geography and sexual preference. Things we thought were not long for this world turned out to be reborn in greater numbers and cultural influence (e.g., biblical inerrancy and fundamentalism).

Having lived through such a protracted debate on how theology is to be done, one is painfully aware that where one starts and how one proceeds become crucial issues. There is irony here: If nothing is self-evident, then anything can be claimed. In such a time it is difficult to argue for a starting point, since *arguing* implies common standards. I am convinced that the biblical scholarship and theological work of the twentieth century constitute a major revolution in the history of Christian faith in the western world. We were enabled to look at the Bible in new ways. We also saw the limitations of doing theology confined to denominational loyalties and documents. Very few had a good idea of what the new world would look like, but it was clear that we were on the verge of something dramatically new. All of this was in the context of the catastrophic violence of the twentieth century and the revolutionary changes in the political and national alignments. It was not a time for business as usual. What was surprising about this changing situation was that it was initiated by the recovery of the sixteenth-century reformers, as well as the ecumenical creeds, all against the background of the renaissance in biblical study. Something new was happening because we were attending to things very old.

Luther and the Priority of Grace

With all these things in mind, and having been granted the gift of living some eighty years in such a world, let me propose to speak of Protestant piety as defined by Martin Luther.[1] This of course produces the inevitable: Why? The simple answer is that reading Luther is a way to re-discover the key to Protestant piety, freed of centuries of interpretation and rivalries.

---

1. The word "piety" can be helpful in reminding us that faith involves trust of the heart, gratitude, joy and even practice, in contrast to intellectual assent to ideas. Luther uses the word faith, but always in this larger sense of piety.

This, however, is not easy. We need to acknowledge that the early sixteenth century is not our world. Between us and that time there is a great divide of five centuries of scientific, political, social, philosophical, and theological change. Luther may have lived at the time of Copernicus, but he was steeped in medieval ways of thinking and practice. Then there is the fact that Luther can be brilliant and determined, as well as stubborn, idiosyncratic, and vitriolic. Any reading of Luther will have to acknowledge this. At the same time, such reading is very complicated. While going back to Luther may free us from our set ideas about what he said, reading Luther from the twentieth and twenty-first centuries allows us to see more clearly what is essential and antithetical to his understanding of Protestant piety.

To understand Luther's view of grace, we shall look at the way it finds expression in writings from 1515-20. This period begins with the *Lectures on Romans*. While there is no agreement as to when the initial break through regarding justification by grace occurred for Luther, it is hard to place it after *Romans*.[2] Here Luther is clear on this matter and is prepared to defend it vigorously against conventional wisdom. Two years later he posts the *Ninety-Five Theses*, which contain his attack on indulgences—a widely successful church practice producing assurance to the faithful as well as financial income for the church.[3] In 1520 two treatises extended his understanding of grace: one was "The Babylonian Captivity of the Church" and the other was "The Freedom of a Christian."[4] The former was especially provocative, since the Mass was the centerpiece of medieval piety. It symbolized the authority of the church to define the sacrament and control its practice by priests, bishops, and Rome itself. In all of these writings the governing idea is grace. There is little development or change in these writings regarding grace, only new applications to church practice and a vision of the Christian life. Moreover, the discussion in *Romans* shows no hesitation or doubt regarding the primacy of grace. In 1515 he has already burned his bridges with Rome by the way he denounces current theology, practice, and church leaders.

Let us begin, then, with the *Lectures on Romans* to see what Luther means by grace. Luther was confronted by Paul's realistic appraisal of the human condition, namely, that all of humanity—Jew and Gentile—have sinned and are unable to fulfill the divine will. More importantly, it was

2. Cf. Oberman, *Luther*, 161–74.
3. Luther, "Ninety Five Theses."
4. Cf. Luther, *Three Treatises*.

clear that Paul saw the good news to be that God redeems the world from sin and the power of Satan by the life, death and resurrection of Jesus Christ. What strikes Luther like a thunderbolt is Paul's declaration that ". . . while we were yet sinners, Christ died for us" (Rom 5:8). For emphasis Paul uses the most threatening word of all to describe what happened in Jesus Christ, namely, the *righteousness* of God. How could Jesus, who died for us, be connected to righteousness, the very symbol of holiness and opposition to sin? This is the revolutionary point: if the righteousness of God is in Jesus, then righteousness does not condemn us, nor does it expect us to save ourselves by endless preparations, acts of remorse, confession, or good works. By his death and resurrection, God declares that righteousness gives life, or to put it simply, we are justified by grace.

But then things get complicated: if this is the case, why has the church spent so much time grounding the gospel in philosophy and proofs for the existence of God, or demanding that we prepare ourselves to be forgiven or engage in meritorious good works, followed by elaborate theories of how the human will cooperates with grace? How can the selling of indulgences or the admonition that we can still do something to assure our salvation be anything other than contrary to Scripture? In effect, if Paul is right, then so much of current religious practice is misleading—dare we even say it is directly opposed to the gospel. Once Luther is convinced that salvation is all about grace rather than the need for human endeavor in the face of condemnation, he launches into his exegesis of Romans, including a continuous stream of criticisms and outbursts against the practices of the church, its priests, and theologians. And he is not polite. It is very hard for him to offer a calm description of God's action in Christ without denouncing what is wrong in the strongest terms.

For Luther, Paul has the authority to turn the world upside because he relies on the prophets' rhetorical strategy of condemning sin as a prelude to proclaiming grace. If Paul dares to do this, the Luther will do the same. So the opening lines of his *Lectures* begin with reference to Jeremiah 1:10:

> The sum and substance of this letter is: to pull down, to pluck up, and to destroy all wisdom and righteousness of the flesh (i.e., of whatever importance they may be in the sight of men and even in our own eyes), no matter how heartily and sincerely they may be practiced, and to implant, establish, and make large the reality of sin (however unconscious we may be of its existence.[5]

5. Luther, *Romans*, 3.

These words are aimed at the theology, rules, and systems of the church, but also at all who follow them because they are given to us by those in authority. In effect, there are things in theory and practice which contradict the proper hearing of the good news. From a theological point of view, if Luther is going to challenge the Pelagian mindset of the church, he will do so only with the authority of Paul. And since he is an Augustinian monk, he will also invoke the name of "blessed Augustine." What better way to begin a discussion of grace, or even launch a critique of conventional wisdom. In one sense, Luther was prepared to engage in a process of clearing away the weeds so that the gospel might flourish—an action H. Richard Niebuhr recommended as the only thing we can do to prepare for the hearing of the gospel.[6]

The opening lines of the *Lectures* clearly indicate that Luther has set his face toward reform, come what may. But they also reflect the hazards of reform and the complications of Luther's life. To begin with, it is not accurate to say that the "sum and substance" of Romans is about destroying and accentuating the reality of sin, when it is about the triumph of grace over sin. Luther will pay dearly for reviving the harsh realism of Augustine and Paul regarding sin. He will be accused of perpetuating the western preoccupation with sin, which generated the elaborate penitential system culminating in the medieval Mass. He will also be charged with destroying the unity of the church.

The problem for Luther was simply this: how can one affirm Paul's theology of grace when church and culture presented an elaborate set of ideas and practices quite to the contrary. If grace has been compromised and distorted, boxed and sold, where is a simple resolution, a mediating position which will not involve challenging the status quo? Whereas current practice domesticated repentance and reduced it to specific actions, culminating in the prayers of the Mass offered as a good work to God, Luther would declare that repentance is a lifelong process and permanent state of the heart.[7] When the church encouraged people to engage in good works, with the assurance that God will accept whatever you can do, Luther was ready to declare that there was nothing we can do but to accept a grace that was totally outside us and offered as a gift by Christ. Given the magnitude of the forces in opposition, both ecclesial and civil, Luther chose the path of a full assault against the powers that be.

6. H. Richard Niebuhr, "Only Way into the Kingdom of God," 447.

7. Luther, "Ninety-Five Theses," 25.

This of course was a dangerous plan, especially when originating from a strong-minded person who was basically an either/or personality. If this approach to things was needed in the warfare with Rome, it did not serve him well in his relations with other Reformers such as Zwingli, and certainly was problematic in his condemnation of Anabaptists and Jews. These are the consequences of his singlemindedness and we will have to come to terms with such excess. We should not, however, accept the modern interpretation of Luther as the champion of individual liberty—a position hard to maintain given his views toward the Anabaptists. Yet the image of Luther refusing to recant before the emperor with his declaration "Here I stand" is part of popular and serious interpretation.[8] What we need to be clear about is that Luther was resolute not because of confidence in himself. In a debate with medieval traditions and the authority of the church, Luther needed more than even an appeal to Augustine and he found this in Scripture.

There is also something ironic about the attack on optimism and works righteousness in the opening lines of *Romans*. Such things were not characteristic of Luther's spiritual life. Quite to the contrary, Luther was beset by an overwhelming sense of unworthiness in the face of the demands of the moral law. He was not an optimist or one who took great confidence in the ability of a person to reform himself by reason or spiritual disciplines. For Luther, given the reality of his sinfulness, the fundamental issue was despair.[9] Consider again the story of his appeal to his mentor in the monastery: When he confessed his inability to reach moral goals and his overwhelming sense of unworthiness in the face of the righteousness of God, he was told to go to the chapel and see the Christ on the cross who died for us.[10] Luther was a person living with the torment of sin. For such a person, Paul's message of grace, quite *apart from the law and all our efforts to present ourselves worthy before God*, was a liberating experience. He already knew he could not save himself. Only the words that Christ died for us "while we were yet sinners" brought peace to his restless soul. This must be kept in mind when he speaks of the freedom of a Christian. We are not free to say or do as we please. But we are free from the need to justify ourselves by achievement and meritorious works and from the crushing despair that robs us of our humanity. Grace liberates us and offers a gift of new life.

8. Ozment, *Age of Reform*, 245.

9. Cf. Luther's preference for the royal road which is between despair and self-righteousness, *Romans*, 137–38.

10. Oberman, 181–83.

One last comment on the opening reference to Jeremiah. Given the prophetic call for repentance and a return to the covenant, as well as Jesus' opening words calling us to repent, Luther could not imagine a reform of the church without first a call for repentance. The fact that Paul uses this strategy in the opening chapters of Romans only strengthened his resolve to endorse it. So also with his understanding of justification by grace: we cannot receive the grace as we are. Grace cannot simply be laid on top of our minds and hearts turned in on ourselves, or a blessing for church or society caught up in self-interest and violence. Grace must first pull down and destroy before it can heal and give new life. This, however, suggested a radically different understanding of sin and grace than what was current in his world.

The Critique of the Medieval Mass

We now need to turn to Luther's critique of the medieval Mass, which reveals other dimensions of his understanding of grace. For reasons that are not clear, it took several years for Luther to connect his view of grace with problems in the Mass. For us, however, it is quite easy to do. Consider the three parts of his critique:[11]

1. The doctrine of transubstantiation: Luther rejected the claim that bread and wine could be changed into the body and blood of Christ (based on the philosophical distinction between essence and accidents, so that the essence changes even though what we see still looks like bread and wine) because it violated the freedom of God. Christ's presence could not be controlled by liturgical practices authorized by the church. Moreover, such practices were without scriptural warrant. Here then was a decisive instance where Luther staked his view on the authority of Scripture over the authority of bishops and tradition.

2. The priority of grace. Liturgical practice claimed that the Mass was our offering to God for our salvation. Even when this was qualified by saying that our offerings are received by Christ who offers his life to God, the movement is still from us to God. But if the Supper signifies God's movement toward us, then the entire sacrament must be

---

11. For Luther's critique of the Mass, cf. "Holy and True Body of Christ," "Treatise on the New Testament, that is, the Holy Mass," "Babylonian Captivity of the Church," and *Large Catechism of Martin Luther*.

re-considered. It now becomes a sign of grace as God's gift to us. Luther was clear: If the Mass is considered a *good work*, then we reaffirm religious legalism, which assumes that our salvation is dependent on our right action, denying the grace of God.

3. Conventional theology held that if the bread and wine become the body and blood of Christ, then the sacrament must work for our salvation by the mere doing of it, as expressed by the Latin phrase *ex opere operato*. This reduced the sacrament to a mechanical or even magical act. By contrast Luther declared that the Word always presents us with a promise of grace, which must be received by faith. We do not create the sacrament. The sacrament is valid because Christ is present as the Word of promise, offering the gift of grace. But it is effective only by our receiving the gift by faith. In fact, he went on to declare that if we eat and drink without faith, hating or mistrusting God, then we eat and drink to our damnation.

By rejecting these aspects of the medieval Mass, Luther struck at the very foundations of the medieval religious system. At the center were bread and wine transformed into the body and blood of Christ. But surrounding it was the church, claiming authority to administer the sacrament. This required priests properly ordained by bishops. The bishops in turn require an imperial church in Rome presided over by one pope, who also oversees right doctrine as the standard for faith and life, as well as interpretation of Scripture. Put simply, to attack the Mass threatened the whole system. Local priests are suddenly deprived of their power to transform simple bread and wine into the body and blood of Christ. Bishops and the pope no longer are needed to control things, nor will they have absolute control if Scripture is affirmed as the primary authority. For good reason the Augustinian monk was dangerous and had to be silenced as soon as possible.

From a biblical perspective, this attack on a practice which infringed on the freedom of God and the sufficiency of God's grace was consistent with major themes in both testaments. One of the distinctive aspects of ancient Judaism was the respect paid to the one, holy and almighty God. Such a God cannot be seen, encapsulated or controlled. God's presence involves mystery and inspires awe. There is always a dialectic of "Yes" and "No," a willingness to be present and a refusal to be manipulated or controlled. Consider the ambiguity of the divine name: God will reveal a name but it shall not be something human beings can control or use for personal gain.

Earthly images and magic are prohibited. Such reverence for the freedom and sovereignty of God does not rule out affirmations of Word and Spirit. A covenant is indeed given, the Torah and specific case laws are provided, with the promise of presence and the sharing of gifts. At the same time, woe to those who forget the covenant or the commandments, for they will face the judgment of God. But even here, those who repent may find forgiveness by the mercy of God, not by burnt offerings and public displays of religiosity.

In the Gospels we could refer to instances where Jesus has little patience for religious practices when they are disconnected from genuine piety. But there are two other passages which speak to the issue of assuming that we can affect our salvation by our achievements. One is 1 Corinthians 1, where Paul lays a trap for the warring Corinthians. On first glance it appears that Paul wants to talk about the Jews and Romans who killed Jesus. But that hardly helps him deal with the problems in Corinth. In reality Paul wants to make the point that Jesus was killed by those making claims to power and wisdom—the very thing the Corinthians are doing to one another. Since Paul knows they affirm that Jesus is the Christ, he can pull the string: you are doing to one another exactly what the rulers of this world did to Jesus. In the initial stage of the argument, the rulers of this world win: Jesus dies on the cross in weakness and foolishness. But when God raises Jesus, God uses the weakness and foolishness of the cross to expose the false power and wisdom of the world. Power and wisdom are supposed to create peace and happiness, not put to death the innocent and righteous. This leads to the final conclusion, namely, that since human claims to wisdom and power too often produce division and death, the cross means an end to all claims. So he concludes, if there is to be any boasting, boast in the Lord.

As I have argued in *Theories of Atonement*, this argument is the only place where the NT deals directly with social/political warfare.[12] It is a devastating argument, stripping warring parties of their claims to privilege and power. Here it is relevant because it parallels the argument in Romans: if in Romans Paul makes the argument that all have sinned and no one has any special claim to standing before God, in 1 Corinthians Paul makes the point that the cross is an end to all human presumption regarding wisdom and power as a basis for special standing. Christians are called to live without claims, because they don't work. The only claim that can truly give life is that in the cross Christ has reconciled us to God and one another.

12. Cf. *Saving Power*, 271–87.

The other passage comes from the Letter to the Hebrews, which makes several elaborate arguments that Jesus is a sacrifice offered to God, greater than any other sacrifice. Moreover, Jesus is our High Priest, greater than all other forms of priesthood. But having made these points to help early Christians understand how and why the anointed one should die, the writer then declares that Jesus' death and resurrection mean *the end of all sacrifice!* (Cf. Heb 8–10) Now the means of reconciliation between God and humanity must be seen in the once-for-all act of Jesus on the cross. It is regrettable that this point is ignored by those in our time wishing to make a case for the Lord's Supper as a re-enactment or re-presentation of Jesus' sacrifice, or even as a perpetual sacrifice.[13] What we have here in Hebrews is the declaration that Christians are to live without any claims to further sacrifice as a means to be reconciled to God, since what God in Christ has done suffices for all time and all places.

From their perspective, both Luther and Calvin were reformers, not originators, recovering the centrality of grace. Against the background of medieval piety, it was revolutionary. Here was the affirmation of salvation by grace rather than human achievement, the possibility of knowing oneself as a sinner yet living without fear. That one might live without claims regarding one's moral or spiritual superiority was shocking. Who could survive such exposure? What would save one from such vulnerability? Following Paul, the only answer was grace: to cease, once and for all, trying to control God but to trust only God.

One way of grasping the full extent of Luther's reform is to think of it as an end to *sacred ritual.* Here I refer to the idea drawn from the study of the history of religions.[14] The word *sacred* is the opposite of profane. It embodies power and value. From this perspective, the world is differentiated by the recognition that there are some objects, places, events, people, and practices which embody something of value and/or divine power. Sacred *rituals* take the next step in providing the means whereby sacred power may be shared or used for specific purposes. Without the sacred there is nothing to share; without rituals there would be no means to share the sacred. We need to note that for people living in the ancient or primitive cultures the sacred is real because it has to do with life and death. It is not something we would call subjective or an invention of culture. Life involves the constant interaction with sacred or life-giving power. Sacred ritual offers the

13. Cf. the discussion of sacrifice in Gift and Promise, 200–28.
14. Cf. Mircea Eliade, *Sacred and Profane* and *Myth of the Eternal Return.*

possibility that we may have access to such sacred power. Over time and when tested by the community, sacred rituals possess the ability to convey sacred power. Religious traditions become important and take on a life of their own because in varying ways they embody the sacred.

What happens, then, if we examine the medieval sacramental practice from the standpoint of sacred ritual? The parallels are striking: objects of this world—bread and wine—are declared to be sacred by action of the priest. As sacred ritual the liturgy gives us a way to offer gifts to God for thanksgiving, aid, and blessings. But such action must be done according to proper form: there are preparatory prayers of repentance to enable believers to approach the altar, prayers for Christ's presence, the consecration of the bread and wine, the breaking of the bread and pouring of the wine, and finally the sharing of the elements. The ritual takes our human efforts and unites them with Christ's work and in return we are allowed to share in the benefits of Christ. Finally, if the ritual follows the proper procedure, involving the transformation of bread and wine into the body and blood of Christ, it works by the doing of it. The ritual automatically produces what it promises. For believers, the argument merely states the obvious: if the ritual contains the body and blood of Christ, then it must have and convey sacred power. How could it not be effective?

Some will take this comparison as simply another form of anti-Roman Catholic prejudice. Let it be said, however, that Luther's point is not simply directed at the medieval Mass, but all Christian claims and practices which seek to confine sacred power to things of this world and use such power for our purposes. Moreover, I would argue that the tendency toward sacred ritual is a *natural tendency* among all forms of piety. How else explain that within one decade of Luther's initial breakthrough, Protestants were arguing among themselves over which practice was most appropriate to speak of Christ's *real presence* and spent some five hundred years excluding one another from the table? In our time Protestants argue over minor changes to liturgies, new hymnody vs. traditional hymnody, and the sanctity of local congregational practice. But they do not restrict the tendency to create sacred rituals to liturgical practice. What shall we make of theological doctrines set aside with such sanctity that agreement determines one's passage to heaven? One could even look at the Protestant tendency to absolutize the Bible, directly parallel to the Roman claim that the pope may speak with infallible words on faith and morals, as another instance of sacred ritual. From national headquarters to local congregations and the words of pastors, there are instances of the attempt to localize sacred power in *some thing, written form, person or practice* and declare that the doing of a certain practice brings saving benefits. And to think we haven't even mentioned the culture wars!

By enlarging our perspective on piety from the stand point of sacred ritual, we gain a much fuller understanding of the magnitude of Luther's revolt. It is not only a rejection of the legalism based on works-righteousness, but a rejection of religion based on sacred ritual which offers believers access to sacred power on demand. The medieval Mass not only sought to contain sacred power in the sacrament, but turned it into a work for our benefit, which is automatically effective. By trying to control God's good pleasure, it compromised the sovereignty of God; by making it something we do rather than God's act toward us, it denied the gracious act of God in Christ. What we have in Luther's critique is no minor quibble about an arcane doctrine regarding bread and wine being transformed into the body and blood of Christ, but the end of a whole system based on the practice of sacred rituals. In this sense his reform is of momentous proportions. It was a challenge to the medieval religious system shaped by the need for holiness and a multitude of forms offered to generate holiness in us by our action, be it prayer, good works, and penance, culminating in the Mass as our offering to God. Whether you begin with justification by grace in *Romans* or the critique of the Mass in *The Babylonian Captivity of the Church*, either document leads to the single idea that it is God who is gracious.

The Protestant Alternative

But what did Luther propose in place of the penitential system and the medieval Mass? Luther offered a theology and practice of the Word, often referring to the *Word of promise*. By this he meant that God's Word is never empty, nor is it merely ideas or information. It is the redemptive power of God which always stands over against us, with us and for us. To speak of such a Word is to proclaim the grace of God in Israel and Jesus Christ.[15] The Word is always a promise to us now, declaring what we may expect. Because God has promised it, we may trust that gifts promised shall be received. Word of promise also meant that the Word also contains a presence. Just

---

15. Luther's treatment of the Ten Commandments, the Lord's Prayer and the sacraments in *The Large Catechism* make it clear that the Word of God is always the Word of grace and central to faith and practice. Cf. *Catechism*, 9–54, 64–79, and 80–100.

as Christ promised a presence in the Great Commission, so in the Lord's Supper he promised to be present in the breaking of bread and pouring of wine. In this sense the Word of promise is not like human promises, which often disconnect the promise from a presence.

When, several years later, Zwingli proposed that the sacrament is an act of remembrance, Luther was furious. He took this to mean the denial of Christ's presence, whereas the Word of promise always includes Christ himself.[16] Luther argued so strenuously for Christ's presence in the Supper because it was a presupposition for the participation in Christ. The point is this: in place of the penitential system culminating in the Mass, Luther would put in its place the proclamation and celebration of the Word of promise as grace and presence; in place of good works as the human response, Luther proposes faith as trust of the heart.

Such faith is always a response to the Word of promise. It does not generate the promise but is called to receive it. So, in regard to the Lord's Supper, Luther will say that the sacrament is valid because of the promise but it is effective only by faith. Such faith is not belief in doctrines or a commitment to good works—all things we can control—but trust in God. It is opening of the self to God in recognition of our incapacity and need. Faith receives and trusts the promise, i.e., the grace and presence of Christ. Conversely, the promise cannot be received without such faith. If the medieval system created practices and forms tied to the penitential system, Luther proceeded to develop practices and forms tied to hearing and celebrating grace: the sermon as the proclamation of the gospel in contrast to the homily; translation of the Bible into the vernacular; a new catechism and hymnody to form hearts and minds, and a new understanding of priesthood. Faith thus stands for our heartfelt response to the Word and it also generates a new form of the church as a community nurturing children and adults in their vocation as Christians.

The polarity of the Word and faith requires further analysis on what is meant by faith and its relation to repentance. Protestants have been ardent in their insistence that faith is itself a gift of the Spirit. Such a claim affirms that by grace the Spirit works in our lives to generate trust. Conversely, this guards against the possibility that we will consider faith as a good work which sets us apart and/or elevates us to special status. But what about repentance? If repentance is a turning to God inspired by the Spirit, then repentance is also a work of grace. On these terms, repentance is not a

16. Cf. Luther, "That These Words," 37:143 and *Catechism*, 95–101.

pre-condition or a work of preparation prior to forgiveness which we create by ourselves. Nor is there a simple chronological order: first you repent and then you believe. (How this relates to the ways liturgies structure the order of repentance and grace will be discussed later.) Grace is not conditional on human efforts to be contrite and/or repent. As understood in the NT, repentance means an admission of sin but also an opening or turning to God without recourse to claims of good works. In Romans and 1 Corinthians we see that the cross nullifies all our striving to save ourselves.

We encounter an illustration of this strange work of grace in the opening selections of Handel's *Messiah*. At the outset the theme of comfort is announced. But then ponder what the Word of comfort will actually do: It will shake the foundations of the earth and all nations. It will purify like a refiner's fire. It is so threatening that we are asked: Who shall abide the day of the Lord's coming? The conjunction of these themes almost defies logic. We move from comfort to the terrifying work of God, followed ultimately by the promise of good tidings to come. This is not a simple three step process, easily understood by our concepts of justice and moral order. In fact, the prophetic vision shatters our expectations. It has a dynamic of its own, first played out in the interplay of holiness and grace in Exodus and Mount Sinai, then repeated in prophetic speech and the Psalms.

The relation of repentance to grace is also exemplified in Jesus' first words in Mark 1:14. First is the announcement of the coming of the kingdom, then the call to repent and believe in the gospel. Can repentance be separated from the new and gracious thing which God is doing? It cannot, nor can it be separated from faith. The same dynamic appears in Paul's devastating rebuke of the Corinthians (1 Cor 1). In their divisions and quarrels, they are replicating the world's claims to wisdom and power which crucified the chosen one of God. Jesus on the cross represents all who suffer for righteousness sake. But God vindicates this Jesus and the righteous, thereby exposing the weakness and foolishness of the rulers of this world. Paul's conclusion is that one must give up all claims which divide and believe in Christ. Here it is evident that repentance is joined with faith: It is to turn from our desire to prove ourselves righteous and claim only Christ. But it is not a work which gains merit, since if it were, we would fall into the contradiction of claiming that in order to be justified by grace we must first make ourselves worthy.

If it is correct to refrain from thinking of repentance as something we do prior to grace, then we are led to the conclusion that repentance and faith are joined together. Both constitute a state of heart and mind, not a once-for-all act. Grace cannot be received without faith as trust of the heart. There must be an opening of the heart to God, or if one prefers, there must be a space in our hearts where we give up reliance on pride and self-love. For faith to trust God, repentance must nullify our striving to save ourselves. Both are the work of the Spirit by grace. This now makes evident why Luther, in the first thesis of the *Ninety-five*, declared that repentance was a life-long process. No doubt he had in mind the fact that the task was enormous! But it is equally correct to interpret Luther to mean that faith incorporates repentance into the life of faith as a permanent orientation. To affirm justification by grace means to also affirm that we always must repent our efforts to turn from God rather than to God, from closing ourselves to grace rather than opening ourselves to grace. This suggests that we must move from the duality of repentance and faith toward the unity of the two. In effect, they must be joined together in something quite new, thereby rejecting the idea that the two exist in us as separate moments in time or separate states of mind.

But how shall we name this new form of piety? Luther does not give us a new word for it but simply speaks of faith. This means we must allow faith to be defined by how it functions in hearing the gospel. Such faith draws repentance into its life so that our trust of God includes remembrance of our sin and the need for repentance. But this faith is not dominated by repentance but is now governed by the assurance of grace, as affirmed in our baptism and the promise of the gospel in Word and table.

We are now at a point to see that the possibility of something new is generated by the new life in Christ. Faith receives, trusts, and celebrates this new life, given as a gift. Christian piety, therefore, is not simply about *our* turning to God or *our* trusting God, but receiving the new life Christ creates on earth. Grace transforms persons and generates a new community in Christ. Consider John's declaration that we must be born again and Paul's claim that in Christ we die and rise with him. In both of these writers, receiving the gift is not a matter of receiving new ideas which we shall use to revive ourselves and chart a new course. Neither Paul nor John understands the new life as giving birth to rational beings capable of living independently from God or others. They think in terms of the transformation of human life by means of our union with Christ. It is a new spiritual existence. So Paul speaks of the body of Christ and John speaks of the vine and branches, as well as the unity of the Father and Jesus and the disciples.

(Cf. John 15–17) All this is implied in Luther's understanding of faith, i.e., to trust God alone and to participate in the new life of Christ. This new life involves union with Christ and union with those bound together in Christ. Community is not something added to the new life, nor is it something we choose. It is not a voluntary association. To receive new life in Christ and live in him means to be joined together with fellow believers.

This brings us to the delicate issue of the nature of this new creation in Jesus Christ. Several things are implied in the way it has been presented. One is that the distinction between justification and sanctification is difficult to maintain. To be sure, we must always affirm that we are justified by God's act and not our efforts. But since repentance and faith are the work of the Spirit in us by grace, a logical or material distinction between justification and sanctification cannot be maintained. In justification grace is already at work in us.

A second point is that from this perspective it is possible to speak of a new being as sons and daughters of God, children of the promise. We are no longer strangers and enemies of God. We do not start over each day as if we were prior to being in Christ—whether you wish to name this by baptism, justification or union with Christ. There is an assurance of faith, grounded in the grace of God, which allows us to rejoice in our union with Christ and membership in the community of Christ. If we were not in a new place defined by union with Christ, then Luther's great work on the freedom of a Christian would make no sense. It would mean that even though we heard the Word of forgiveness yesterday or this morning, we really are not free but still live under the shadow of judgment. But freedom would not be the only casualty. This would also mean the end of joy and a return to the treadmill of wondering if God really loves us.

The last point is the reminder that the reality of the new life in Christ never means the absence of sin or the struggle between sin and grace. Faith incorporates repentance into its life because in this life we are always sinners on the way. There is no room for utopian designs, but just as important, there is no room for despair. One might risk saying that in general we have done fairly well stamping out utopian designs; perhaps far more attention needs to be given to the new reality of grace which takes away despair.

To close the discussion of the Protestant alternative, we need to consider Luther's images of the freedom of a Christian and the priesthood of all believers. From one perspective, these images continue to dismantle the medieval world. If grace bestows freedom, then the elaborate system of sacraments and works, with the attending structures of the church, were called into question. If all are priests, then the vertical hierarchy from God to pope and kings, through the religious and secular is leveled. But if you dismantle the old world, what will you put in its place?

Bear in mind the medieval world sought to unite all things in one grand scheme. But there were serious cracks. Even a simple one—the withholding of the cup from the laity—pointed to the division of the spiritual from the physical and religious orders from the laity in the secular world. A more subtle issue was the goal of our love. Augustine had deferred his conversion, assuming that love of God was in opposition to love of the world. Was love of God and the world an either/or? Could one love both, or even love all things in God? In effect, not only was the world divided between religious and secular, so was the human heart in its choice of love. Luther's two images offered a new way of thinking about identity/vocation and the church.

If grace confers freedom, then the Christian is free from the endless obligations to prove oneself and the rules of the church. But less one think Luther is opening the door to libertarianism, he declares that those free in Christ are the servants of all.[17] To be free does not mean separation but the embrace of the neighbor in the community of Christ.[18] Likewise, the priesthood of all believers rejected the vertical separation of the religious from the laity and envisions a church where all are called to serve by virtue of their baptism.[19] This conferred an equality and unity not possible in the old system. If all are priests and priests can marry and be in the world, then all things may be loved in God. If all are priests, then all bring to the altar their work and their work is sanctified in a new way. Suddenly the division of religious and secular is healed. The spiritual and physical are not antithetical but are joined in faith, love and work. One does not choose to serve God or humanity, church or the world, but one is called according to the gifts given. In a most profound way, the Protestant alternative is a call to unify all things in grace.

17. Luther, "Freedom," 277.

18. The contrast between such freedom and the modern idea of freedom which sets the individual against others and the community could not be stronger.

19. Luther, "Freedom," 289–92.

The Subversion of Grace

It is not easy to practice a religion of grace. What appears with such joy and freedom is easily compromised. Here I gather together several examples of the way grace is subverted. They are included here because we live in a world where our core affirmations are always contested and threatened. It is also the case that by working through contentious issues we understand such affirmations in a new way and establish guidelines for faith and practice.

1. The Older Brother

The parable of the prodigal son stands as the great witness to God's grace. (Luke 15:11–32) Along with the parable of the laborers in the vineyard, Jesus gives us a dramatic presentation of how God transforms the world. But in the story of the prodigal, Jesus complicates this example of grace by introducing a third character, the older brother. He is not happy. His words suggest jealousy and resentment, perhaps simmering for years. It would be easy to focus on the nuances of sibling rivalry and family systems. But the story is not a brief outline for a modern novel on how parents spoil children, or rivalries between brothers. So why add the brother to the story? The older brother speaks for our expectation that the good are to be rewarded and the evil punished. From this perspective the father shows disrespect for hard work and faithful service, thereby violating the moral standard of retributive justice. Those who break the law should be punished, not rewarded. By adding the older brother to the story, Jesus tells us he knows our discomfort with grace and challenges our conventional moral wisdom. The older brother speaks for us.

The parable becomes a frontal assault on conventional moral standards, based on retributive justice, which leave people to suffer what they deserve. In religion, such legalism insists that our relation to God is determined by what we do. In one sense it is great heresy of biblical religions. God calls us to be holy and therefore only the holy, determined by moral rules and regulations, may stand before God. In every age all branches of Christianity have witnessed tendencies in this direction. Even the admission that all have sinned has not prevented us from separating the good from the bad, or the truly repentant (i.e., who may come to the Lord's Supper) from those who lack true contrition or do not believe as we do. The practical benefit of legalism is that it tells us what we have to do to be acceptable to God, when we have done it, and how we may take comfort in God's approval. It even goes so far as to plant the idea that we deserve what we get because of our accomplishments and good deeds

Jesus meets many people who are faithful and who love God and neighbor. He also meets some who have succumbed to legalism. "Good teacher, what must I do to inherit eternal life?"(Mark 10:17) Can we do a good work on the Sabbath when rest is commanded? Even the seemingly innocent question "Who is my neighbor?" reflects the self-serving influence of legalism. (cf. Luke 10: 29–37) If we can answer that question, then we will also know who is *not* my neighbor and know when to stop our works of love. Jesus refuses to get drawn into such discussions. Have you noticed that he never answers the question which leads to the parable of the Good Samaritan, but simply gives an example of a person who *is* a good neighbor? Such questions also prompt Jesus to give sayings which summarize the Law as the double commandment of love (drawn from Deuteronomy), or re-state the laws in contrast to what was said of old. At other times he simply tells parables.

The parable of the prodigal son is an image of the gospel itself: in a world where we can never get beyond mistakes and failures, where some are excluded by birth and class, where many have no means to present themselves as persons who have fulfilled the law, Jesus proposes that our standing before God is not based on what we do but on God's grace to heal, make whole, and give life to those who appeared dead. It is a new world where one lays down his life for his friends, where a good person dies for sinners, and where God vindicates the crucified by raising him up to be Lord and, most important, where God chooses not to destroy a world which kills the righteous. St. John considers these events and can only conclude that "God so loves the world . . ." Paul cannot stop talking about a grace which justifies and gives life. The parable of the prodigal is more than praise of the love of God. It goes to the heart of what is happening in the lives of the listeners. It is all about our relation to God, who will transform the world. But we need to be careful: too often the older brother and all the tendencies toward legalism are lifted up as examples of Jews. We need to affirm that legalism is a part of being human and appears in every time and place. It is in us. Those who take holiness seriously are especially vulnerable. Therein lies the reason we must take the older brother seriously. He fails to see that God wills to restore and redeem.

2. A Misguided Theory of Atonement

From start to finish the theory of penal substitution is misguided. In an effort to explain why Jesus died, the theory assumes that God can only act in accordance with the demands of retributive justice. Since sin has offended God, God requires the death of an innocent to settle accounts. Therefore Jesus dies, God is satisfied, and Jesus is able to share the benefits of his offering to God with those who believe. The problem is that it is simply wrong. Why?

First, it starts and ends entirely in a legalistic framework where it is all about legal requirements. Even though Jesus may die out of an act of love for us, God grants forgiveness only because the law has been fulfilled. In effect, God is passive, waiting to be appeased.

Second, it is contrary to the NT. At no point does the NT say that God requires the death of an innocent to atone for the sins of the world. There is no system of sacrifice where a death is offered to appease God. The Paschal Lamb is not a sacrifice for sin and on the Day of Atonement the animal is led out of the city to "take away" our sin, not offered as a sacrifice to God. The NT does say that Jesus dies because of sin, that Jesus dies as a sacrifice for us, and that Jesus' death shows forth the love of God. But at every point Jesus dies out of his fidelity to God and God vindicates him in his resurrection. The NT is clear: God is not passive but the active one who redeems the world.

We should also note that it does not solve the problem by arguing that humans are not appeasing God because it is the trinitarian Son who offers his life to God the Father. This does not avoid appeasement but only elevates it to the level of the Trinity. Why should God the Father require such from God the Son? Penal substitution subverts the gospel of grace, turning the story of Jesus into a legal bargain or exchange: Jesus agrees to die and God agrees to rescind the judgment. Thus in the end we are still dealing with a meritocracy based on moral achievement. This theory has had an enormous effect on faith and practice, since it undergirds the medieval Mass and much of Protestant worship and piety. Fortunately, many Protestant liturgies are no longer relying on it as the basis for the Lord's Supper. But it still casts a legalistic shadow over much theology of the cross.[20]

20. For a fuller discussion of sacrifice and penal substitution, see the discussions in *Saving Power*, chapters 1 and 3.

3. What Ever Happened to Compassion?

For several decades I have observed the absence of compassion in religious and public discourse. This is of concern since, in traditional Protestant piety, compassion would be a sign of the grateful heart redeemed by grace. If gratitude is the engine driving our love of God and neighbor, compassion would be its sign. So how does one explain that too often the poor receive a stone rather than a loaf of bread? The simplest answer would be to see the problem as just another form of our legalism. Once again the older brother wins. But in this case, it would appear that a crucial substitution has been made which nullifies compassion. Recall that faith as trust of the heart is the proper response to grace. But what if something has gone wrong with faith? What if faith has become a work and grace received is a reward for our faith. The benefits of Christ thereby take on a different meaning: instead of being gifts they are what we have earned by our believing in right doctrine or the performance of good works.

If that seems to be stretching things, consider William Evans' discussion of federal theology. Evans presents a conclusion by Perry Miller that it was possible for a covenant theology to change the gospel of grace into a grand bargain. The covenant was the attempt to ". . . provide a ground for assurance of salvation and a foundation for ethical exhortation." In effect, the covenant became a conditional contract, based on a bargain: if we believe, God must save us.[21] Evans is quick to admit that not all historians agreed with Miller. The point, however, is not to take sides in an historical debate but to have us consider the unthinkable, namely, the possibility of inverting the gospel of grace into a form of legalism where I rest secure in God's grace toward me because of my faith. In effect, legalism can lead to the conclusion that we deserve the grace of God and thereby invert, convert or subvert even the very meaning of grace.

Lest this discussion be used for partisan purposes, I would argue that it occurs in both conservative and liberal traditions. For example, if one already is living in a conservative world, where the legal framework of penal substitution predominates, then it is but a short step to see Christ earning our salvation and we received it by faith and a promise to live according to ecclesial norms. The subversion occurs right here. Our action is the key for being part of the community of Christ and sets us apart from unbelievers. In the liberal version, the love of God frees us from ignorance and

21. Evans, *Imputation*, 59.

repressive traditions so we might create new life on earth. Individuals are thereby given a new status, based on their ability to free themselves from false ideas about God and themselves. We are able to reform ourselves and may take credit for it. Since faith frees the individual, there is little need to speak of an ongoing process of repentance because we already embody the ideal and may re-order life accordingly. In the end, we make ourselves so that faith as trust in God and a life of repentance are unnecessary.

In either version of this subversion of faith, what happens becomes all the more possible when one adds to this discussion the long-standing claim of American innocence. No matter what the historical record shows, bad things and/or social evils never happened. We are all innocent and deserve whatever we have received in this new world. The end product is the absence of compassion. Could Christian faith be subverted in any more dangerous way? Not only is grace denied, but the link between grace and compassion is destroyed. If this can happen in Protestant communities founded on an evangelical message of grace, then something is wrong and we need to admit that we have some unfinished business.

4. The Shadow of the Medieval Framework

We have already reviewed Luther's critique of the medieval Mass. But in spite of his affirmation of grace, most Protestant liturgies retain what I would call the *medieval framework*. By this I refer to a general movement from repentance for sin, remembrance of Christ's death, the elevation of bread and wine as signs of body broken and blood poured out, and the plea for mercy just before receiving the bread and wine. Prior to recent decades, this framework would include a theology of penal substitution, to the exclusion of most other theories of atonement such as reconciliation, liberation, restoration and the renewal of creation. In effect, the Lord's Supper has been turned into a sacrament of penance, which is all about repentance and sin, Christ's death offered to a just God in exchange for forgiveness. When the service reaches the high point of forgiveness of sins in the sharing of bread and wine, the service ends abruptly with a prayer, hymn and blessing. In one Protestant service the Prayer of Thanksgiving takes thirty-five seconds. What this means is that there is no time given to celebration of the new life we have in Christ and with one another, no time for actually rejoicing in the moment. We are sent out and expected to return and repeat the same service. In other words, we start each service at the same place. No wonder people ask why there is no joy.

Luther envisioned a celebration of the Word of grace, leading to the affirmation of joy and freedom. Calvin offers a wonderful image of the Supper: It is like a father, who has already blessed the family with gifts, now convenes the family again to bestow more blessings.[22] The key here is that there can be no joy in the Supper if it is all about sin, repentance and pleading for mercy. There can be no real celebration of life if most of the time is spent reminding ourselves and God that we failed and betrayed God. Time is important, in relations with one another and in the liturgy as we hear the Word and respond in prayers. For there to be joy there must be both the reality of grace and the time to celebrate it. The medieval framework gives a nod to grace, but the predominant theme is our unworthiness and the suffering it has caused, ending in a declaration of momentary forgiveness. It is time to reclaim the Supper as a proclamation and celebration of grace. Both need more time.

The question running through all four examples of the subversion of grace is: Will the older brother win. When all is said and done, will Christian faith be reduced to the two great embodiments of the older brother: The first is moral and religious legalism, which claims that we are righteous either by our actions or our faith. The second is American optimism, which claims that we liberate ourselves by our reason or action. Both create a world of religious meritocracy, where by our action we get what we deserve. Both mean an end to compassion since both subvert Protestant piety.

This then is the starting point for faith: The Word of promise which is always grace. Protestant piety was born in this declaration of good news. It is nurtured and endures only by returning again and again to that Word of promise. In this sense it generates an unusual form of spirituality: it lives by trust in God alone and is suspicious when trust is placed in worldly things and even ecclesial authorities. It is willing to speak of faith as a journey, as in *Pilgrim's Progress*, but cautious about spending too much time talking about ourselves. If there is to be meditation or contemplation, it must begin with the cross, from which emanates the grace of God. Such faith is ultimately transformed by the Spirit in ways we can never imagine. It also draws us into community, which brings us to the next chapter.

22. Calvin, *Institutes*, 1359–60.

2

Community

A. Grace and Community

GRACE AND COMMUNITY ARE inseparable. Community first appears in the generative power of God to create that which is not God but which exists only by the power of God's life-giving Spirit. It is a vast world of boundless variety and amazing interdependency, as is evident to the writer of Psalm 104. In such a world of life and death, human beings take their place, sharing in the wonders and goodness of God's creation. While blessed with certain gifts which distinguish them, they are intentionally part of the creation. They do not live outside it, nor are they left there by accident or for reason of punishment. They are not abandoned on a desert island, waiting to be rescued. They are the stuff of the earth to enjoy life with God and one another. Against all Manichaean mistrust of the creation, what God creates is declared good (cf. Gen 1). God has made it all in wisdom, all of it expresses God's glory and God rejoices in it (Ps 104: 24, 31). In such a world there is a unity of means and ends: the means embody and contain the end, even while pointing to larger goals.

Grace generates community meant for life. That life, in the case of humans, is complex and varied. There is no simple diagram which can portray the interconnections between God, humanity, and the rest of the created order. Nor can we give priority to one aspect, as if the others can be subordinated or denied. For example, in a time of ecological crisis, the stories of creation in Genesis 1–2 are faulted for the priority given to human beings. In the first account humans are the final act of creation, blessed and given authority to subdue and have dominion over the earth. Such language, however, is hardly a mandate to pillage and destroy for monetary gain, since the overall vision is one where human beings are part of the created order, which is repeatedly declared to be good. There is no doubt that the progression of the six days of divine work gives pre-eminence to humans, but that is balanced by the fact that humans are not created in isolation but along with living creatures on the sixth day and only after five days of wondrous work by the beneficent Creator. There is an order here, but it is hardly the story of unlimited power of humans set against nature. Rather it is a providential order which oversees the entire creation. Human dominion is given by the God who still claims possession of the whole creation (cf. Ps 95). This sense of humans being a part of creation emerges vividly in the second account, where it specifically says that God "put him in the garden of Eden to till it and keep it" (Gen 2:15). Human beings do not live above the creation but in it, nor may they pretend to be God, a point made clear by the warning not to claim divine knowledge (Gen 2:16–17).

The interconnectedness—and precarious nature—of our life with God, the creation, and one another is further illustrated in the second vision of creation, in the creation of the male and then the female. In spite of the fanciful two-step process of creation, as well as the patriarchal bias built into the structure, there is a crucial affirmation present here which should not be overlooked: human beings are made for life with one another. This assertion is contained in God's acceptance without hesitation of the fact that human beings need one another for all sorts of things, including enjoyment of one another and procreation. Put in simple terms, while human beings are made for love and loyalty to God, this creator God is not offended or annoyed by the fact that human beings need, want, love, and desire one another as well as God. Even this is blessed by God. To be sure, the writers already know that things can and will go wrong, that is, the possibility of wrong choices based on loving what we ought not to love. Yet even while knowing this, Genesis 2 gives us an unimaginable description of paradise, where exposure and vulnerability do not arouse fear. It concludes: "And the man and his wife were both naked, and were not ashamed"(Gen 2:24–25). Here we have the affirmation that we are made for community marked by trust and peace with God, with one another and with the created order.

Most importantly, the betrayal of trust toward any one of these destroys the harmony between all.

Grace is also the power to repair the damage done by ill will and violence. Grace restores life rather than increasing the things which destroy life. Even the grace which liberates us from destructive communities aims for the restoration of communities of grace. This is the case in ancient Israel and in the church formed by Jesus Christ. At the heart of Israelite religion is the creation of a community from diverse peoples liberated from bondage and united in a covenant named for Moses. This community was based on oaths by God and the people to be faithful to one another. It was given a structure expressed in the Decalogue to hold back chaos. The detailed rules for daily life became part of the Law, as testimony that God did indeed intend to create a community on earth which would endure over time. While Israelite history is filled with betrayal and disloyalty on the people's part, there was always a call to return to the covenant. What was founded by grace was always renewed by grace, or to use the words of the Psalms, God's loving kindness. Most important, as later generations interpreted the covenant, it was celebrated as a relation of personal loyalty and love toward God and neighbor (cf. Deuteronomy).

A similar logic appears in the new covenant formed by Jesus as he gathered followers with the proclamation of the kingdom of God. It was given ritual form by the last supper, which by his resurrection became the Lord's Supper. It was a celebration of his presence and the new community formed by our life in him and in the Spirit. If the synoptic Gospels emphasize the language of discipleship (repent, believe, follow, serve, take up your cross, deny yourself, preach, teach, baptize and look for the coming kingdom), St. John and St. Paul give us organic images to emphasize the transformation of believers and their dependency on Christ: rebirth, living water, the bread of life and vine and branches as well as dying and rising and the body of Christ. The language of discipleship and the language of new life are consistent with one another because each language assumes a new community created by grace. Community is a gift and a promise: it originates in what God does in and through Jesus Christ in spite of our resistance; it is sustained only by our participation in the new life of Christ.

B. The Revival of Reformation Theology

As we discovered in our discussion of grace, the revival of Reformation theology in the twentieth century had a major impact on centric Protestants. It meant a new emphasis on the Bible, the creeds, Augustine, as well as Luther and Calvin. Suddenly Karl Barth was talking about the strange world of the Bible in a commentary on Romans, while the next decade brought Reinhold Niebuhr turning away from liberal optimism in favor of Augustinian realism, talking about an impossible possibility.[1] The new starting point was precipitated by WWI, which came to symbolize the collapse of claims to reason as well as the moral and religious values of the liberal tradition. What emerged was the reintroduction of biblical language and the Christology of the creeds and Reformers.

This shift toward the Reformers changed the way community was understood. To begin with, the new perspective meant that the community, rather than the individual, was given primary status. To speak of God meant to speak of the God of the covenants and prophetic speech aimed at restoration of community. We were reminded that Jesus' great commandment was embedded in the bonds between a faithful people and God (cf. Deuteronomy). If this was the case, then Jesus' teachings and mighty deeds had to be placed in the context of his reference to the kingdom of God and the new covenant made in his death and resurrection. The shape of salvation was now recast in communal terms, with the originating community being the unity of Christ with believers. In this way the priority of grace leads directly to the priority of community. This becomes apparent in the Pauline emphasis on participation in Christ, whereby believers die and rise in Christ and have life only in Christ and in the Spirit. The Gospel of John makes the same point by means by introducing transformative and organic images. We we are born again, our relation to Christ is like that of a vine and its branches, we receive living water and the bread of life. We also participate in the circle of love which extends from God the Father to the Son to the disciples, so that the world might know and love God.

Just as important, these communal images are placed in an historical context. God is in process of redeeming the world and moving it toward an eschatological goal. What originates in grace culminates in a community on earth called to demonstrate God's purpose for the entire world. To participate in Christ is to be reconciled to God and to one another and to

1. Cf. Niebuhr's *Moral Man.*

44

be agents of reconciliation. The key here is that the church has a vocation and it flows from its being in Christ. Baptism and the Lord's Supper are no longer secondary symbolic gestures but signs and seals of the new reality. In this sense the Great Commission is illustrative of the life of the church: While present in their midst, Christ commands them to make disciples, baptize and teach with the assurance of his continual presence to the end of time. Christ is never an absentee director of operations nor are we left alone to figure it out. Jesus does not engage in long-distance learning, but communicates new life as the Lord in our midst. Such comments point to why the real presence of Christ in the Lord's Supper was so essential for both Luther and Calvin.

The new way of speaking of Christ and church is illustrated by the celebration of the peace of Christ. When we affirm the peace of Christ we declare that there is a new way of being in this world. We are at peace with God and one another because of what God has done in Christ. It is a safe place amidst the violence of this world. When this safe place becomes a place of violence, then the peace of Christ is betrayed and the community must be reconstituted by repentance and trust. The peace of Christ also determines the relations between members. These relations are derived directly from our presence at the table. It is in Christ we discover unity, not based on our agreement but God's act in Christ. Unity is neither an achievement nor something reached by our negotiations. Indeed, in our time we have discovered that the church of agreement is dead. Unity exists as a gift of Christ. In a similar way, there is equality between those at the table. Here again, equality is not conferred or granted by the state, the church, traditions, family status or those in power. God created us as part of the human family and in Christ God has claimed us again as sons and daughters.

Both unity and equality have been denied and abused for centuries in the church and societies where Christian faith has been dominant. The sorrowful history of American culture and churches reveals this to be true. In such situations the gospel is both judgment and hope: a Word of judgment exposing the violations of our unity and equality in Christ while at the same time calling us to actualize what is already present in the peace of Christ. Centric Protestants make no claim to have overcome all of the failings of the church in this regard. What does mark them is a willingness to acknowledge the violations and consider how our faith and practice may be reformed by the grace of God.

What is especially important is that the same paradox of sin and grace, represented by the idea of justification by grace, applies to the religious community. It too suffers the pains of our fallen state. It cannot claim innocence or perfection, nor pretend to be an extension of the incarnation. In this life we still struggle with the power of sin even while we celebrate the new life in Christ. Therefore there are limits to what we may claim for the present or for the future regarding the community. We may not claim perfection or attempt, by one great leap forward, to escape the limits of our life for a utopian dream. The limits we face are of two sorts and it is significant to note the difference: one set relates to our finitude, which may not be equated with sin or evil. We do not possess absolute knowledge, power or goodness by virtue of our physical limits and the limits of space and time. Claims to absolute truth are always tempting but must be resisted, be it over doctrine, moral principles or the Bible itself. The other set of limits pertains to our sinfulness: we love our selves more than we ought and accordingly see the world in terms of partial and self-serving goals. Even our very best efforts are not free from self-interest. To make things worse, we live in historic and social networks of self-interest, which incorporate long standing rivalries and divisions. The truth is that even the churches may not claim innocence. Whether one names this general perspective as Pauline or Augustinian, it is the moral realism affirmed in the reformers and revived in the last century. As a consequence, the celebration of the freedom and grace of the gospel always contains the provision that individuals and communities are in need of repentance.

By the 1950s a new generation of leaders was forced to address a serious problem: what is the relation of sacrificial love to coercive power—be it violent or non-violent coercion? The former generation had supported the allies in WWII, thereby affirming the need for violent coercion in extreme circumstances. But following that war the tension between love and power still remained within churches. For his part, Reinhold Niebuhr had exposed the problem and simply affirmed a twofold ethic: the highest moral value was sacrificial love, but the demands of social justice required the use of coercion. Always wanting to turn the tables on his critics, he was quick to point out that Gandhi was in fact not a disciple of non-coercion but non-violent coercion.[2] The economic and political pressure brought against the British forced the empire to change. Niebuhr could therefore argue that Gandhi supported his position rather than contradicted it: in this world

2. Niebuhr, *Moral Man*, cf. 241–56.

social justice can only be achieved by coercive power, though non-violent coercion was preferable. This empowered many social and political leaders, but it left unresolved the exact relation of sacrificial love and power in the life of Christians. The next generation, however, quickly responded.

In the late 1950s, a young black pastor by the name of Dr. Martin Luther King, Jr. organized a political movement using non-violent coercion to achieve civil rights for people of color. It drew on the analysis and strategies found in Niebuhr's 1932 manifesto: *Moral Man and Immoral Society*: first, the validation of coercion in a society which used power to segregate and oppress minorities; second, the superiority of non-violent coercion on moral and strategic grounds. King refused to see this strategy as a concession to political necessity but as a Christian strategy.[3] In this sense, the civil rights movement bridged the gap between love and power. This development was soon joined by the liberation theologies which connected the sufferings of oppressed people with the sufferings of Jesus and the call for liberation. Jürgen Moltmann (1965) placed this in the context of an eschatological vision.[4] James Cone published a Black liberation theology in 1969, while Gustavo Gutiérrez (1971) presented a theology of liberation from a Roman Catholic perspective.[5] In the cases of Moltmann and Gutiérrez, the traditional affirmations of Trinity, incarnation, sin and salvation were marshalled to think about salvation as liberation from the oppressive powers of this world. This was extremely important: liberation of oppressed people was not based on liberal assumptions drawn from the culture, but the incarnation of God in the midst of human suffering. Cone, by contrast developed a Black theology of liberation over against the white church, growing out of the black experience. Feminist liberation theology developed in a variety of ways by race and sexual orientation, seeking to find a distinctive perspective over against centuries of patriarchal domination.[6]

While liberation theologies called for bold changes in faith and practice, it is hard to imagine their origin without the revival of theological and biblical themes in the previous generation. By going beyond the first generation, liberation theologies changed the vocabulary of theology and our expectations for thinking about the relation of church and world. For

3. Cf. King, Jr. "Letter."

4. Cf. Moltmann, *Theology of Hope*.

5. Cf. Cone, *Black Theology* and Gutierrez, *Theology of Liberation*.

6. For an initial survey of feminist views, cf. Letty M. Russell, ed. *Feminist Interpretation of the Bible*.

one thing, it was now imperative to speak of salvation as more than forgiveness of sins of individuals, or as a promise of heaven, but as reconciliation, liberation, and a new heaven and earth. If the grace of empowerment is as important as the grace of forgiveness, then communities of faith are called to resist oppressive forces. From this perspective, Christian communities are not under obligation to suffer passively, but to restore life in the world and in the church. Ecclesial communities torn apart by ill will and violence need to be restored to the peace of Christ.

The argument, then, is that the view of community among centric Protestants has been shaped by several generations of theology from WWI to the present. As a result, such Protestants find themselves opposed to the authoritarian tendencies among Roman Catholics and conservative Protestants on the one hand, and a liberal culture which has been formed by individualism and moral optimism. This places in perspective some of the longstanding rivalries between centric Protestants and all of these groups. They are unable to endorse the absolute claims of churches regarding Bible, doctrine or episcopal authority, or the attempts to preserve and protect the social status quo which wishes to perpetuate divisions by race, class, and gender. At the same time they reject the attempts to reduce Jesus to moral teachings or separate religion or Jesus from the community of faith. They are open to radical criticism of institutional life, but refuse to give up on the church as the community of Christ. The openness to a realistic view of the limits of doctrine and church rested upon the shift to a christological focus wherein Christ takes precedence over church, tradition and even the Bible.

What sustains the church in such tragic times as these is the paradoxical claim of the gospel: the church is an earthen vessel, subject to doubt, failure and sinfulness, but by the grace of God it lays claim to the treasure of the gospel. The paradox of sin and grace means that we can and must face the truth and that the truth will not destroy us because the last word is a Word of grace. So it is by grace that the church embodies new life and is called to demonstrate the new life God intends for the world. When Protestants are true to their origin, they affirm that the church cannot control or limit the treasure, but the church is called to be and do those things which show forth God's grace. In the present moment of weakness, centric Protestants must regain the confidence and courage to witness to that treasure.

C. Forms of the Church

While making a case for a view of the church among centric Protestants, it is extremely important to acknowledge that the treasure of the gospel takes form in the world in different ways. In part this is because forms of the church reflect strategies to transform the world. If you have never considered baptism as a strategy to change the world, read again the liturgy for this sacrament. Not only is a person claimed by God and incorporated into the people of the new covenant, but parents and god-parents are asked to renounce the evils of this world! (I have always wondered what would happen if at that point in the service we asked which evils they were prepared to renounce.) Or consider the mandates of the Great Commission: teaching, making disciples and baptizing are the ways the church takes form and also the way the church communicates the power of salvation to the world.

Such a view of churches was not my initial assumption. In my work on theories of atonement I considered the possibility that Christian traditions were differentiated by their use of different theories of atonement. Unlike Gustaf Aulén, who proposed that there were three theories, I proposed that there were far more because grace takes different forms in relation to different human needs.[7] But it soon became apparent that specific images of Christ, or theories of atonement, were not the decisive factor in producing different forms of the church. Consider for a moment that many traditions appeal to some form of substitutionary atonement while still holding diametrically different views of the church. This prompted a counter-proposal: What differentiates traditions is the different ways saving power is embodied and communicated to believers. But behind this statement lies the matter of the presence of Christ. What is at stake in different forms of the church is the way traditions affirm the presence of Christ. For some that becomes a debate about real presence in the sacrament of the table, but for others it becomes a debate over Christ's presence in community or with the faithful in the world. All of which is to say that all Christians affirm a *real presence* of Christ, only they do it in different ways. Christ is the vital center and churches differ in the ways they name the time and place for meeting such presence. Consider these six ways of defining the church in relation to the vital center, i.e., ways in which the grace of Christ is communicated to believers.[8]

7. Cf. Gustaf Aulén, *Christus Victor* and my discussion in *Saving Power*, 125, 195, 210–11, 314.

8. This typology of the church first appeared in *Christ the Reconciler* and then was expanded in *Defining the Church for our Time*. It was proposed as an alternative to that

1. Sacramental Participation in the Community of Christ

The strength of this form is participation in the new life in Christ by means of worship and sacraments, supported by ordained ministry, creeds and tradition, which tie the community to the story of Jesus. When the sacraments are increased to seven, they provide a religious structure for all of life. The risk is that the sacraments become ends in themselves. There is also the danger of authoritarian structures with a strong emphasis on sacred rituals and events, leading to a division of the sacred and secular.

2. The Word of Promise Received by Faith

This form directs attention to the proclamation of the good news and our response of trust of the heart, leading to gratitude and service. Preaching, teaching, the catechism, study of Scripture, hymnody, fellowship and service are vital parts. It has also been marked by the priesthood of all believers, the nurture of the community, as well as the sovereignty of God over all worldly structures, including the church. But the emphasis on faith has too often been translated into right belief, be it doctrine or Bible, as well as moral codes, leading to authoritarian structures.

3. Rebirth in the Spirit.

If rebirth in the Spirit is the norm, then the emphasis will fall on the freedom of God to generate new spiritual life rather than giving precedence to tradition and formal structures. This can lead to a very fluid and changing community as members claim the Spirit, or to a reliance on traditions which have served the community in maintaining genuine spiritual life.

4. The Gathered Church as a Disciplined Community set apart from the World.

Here the emphasis falls on the creation of a new, reconciled community, with its traditions of worship, discipline, fellowship, witness and service. Examples may be drawn from Roman Catholic orders, Protestant gathered

of Avery Dulles, *Models of the Church*, where the models are primarily conceptual rather than real churches and where all the models are not considered to be valid. Cf. *Defining the Church*, 121–33.

churches, Anabaptist communities as well as Black churches. As such they offer a powerful witness to new life in actual communities that exist over time. Though they may appear as set apart from the world, they often demonstrate a powerful witness for transforming the world. To the extent that they live apart from the world, they face problems of isolation and the dangers of legalism and division.

5. Acts of Love and Justice in Response to the Call of Christ.

Without denying the role of faith, sacraments or traditions, this form envisions a community that gives priority to acts of love and justice (Matt 25). While this form is represented by the activism of liberal Protestants, it also appears in the Roman Catholic teaching regarding the poor and conservative Protestants who make certain moral concerns a mark of faithfulness. It has traditionally faced two problems: the temptation to make absolute claims about goals and strategies, which may appear as claiming a higher moral righteousness; the risk of cutting itself off from those forms and practices which sustain and nurture faith for the longer journey. Either problem has tended to isolate its members from those in other forms of community.

6. Solidarity with Christ Who Suffers with the Oppressed for Freedom and Justice.

This form draws on the NT and creedal imagery of Jesus coming to liberate those who suffer oppression. The Roman Catholic version can be very orthodox in theology but radical in practice. Among Protestants it appears among liberal activist groups, Black and feminist theology as well as those demonstrating for peace and environmental concerns. It faces the challenge of connecting its strategies for change with the shared traditions of other forms of the church. In the last fifty years it has been a work in progress and there have been great gains in expanding our vision of the transforming power of grace.

For centuries we have treated these different forms of grace as mutually exclusive, assuming that one's preferred form was that mandated by Scripture, tradition and our experience. This analysis of different forms assumes that each represents something essential regarding the way saving power is communicated. In other words, they are not mutually exclusive. If this is correct, then it is time to ask how they relate to one another and whether a complete form of the church would integrate all of these six forms.

The first thing to recognize is that in many ways this has already happened and is happening among centric Protestants. From the beginning, Protestants claimed Word and faith as the dominant form, but included in that a delicate balance of pulpit and table. Since WWII the inclusion of aspects of other forms into the dominant form of Word and faith has increased, due to ecumenical movements, shared theological education, clergy moving between denominations as well as personal preferences and social events. We also need to consider that something of the six forms is in each of us. This also suggests that every congregation probably has members leaning toward other forms besides the dominant form. For example, a Lutheran or United Methodist church may in general be classified as representing the form of Word and faith, but I would venture to say that they contain members leaning toward the sacramental, acts of love and justice, the gathered church—and would you believe it—the charismatic. This should not surprise us since all six forms are rooted in scripture and tradition, just as human personalities reflect different ways of communicating, responding to the gospel and finding meaning. If some members just love sermons while others are overwhelmed by the Lord's Supper and yet others by service and witness in the world, perhaps we need to take note in thinking about the how worship, study, fellowship, evangelism and service are organized.

The fact is that the six forms display different ways of dealing with the essentials needed for the life of the church. Take for example the distinction between being and doing, or that of the church gathered and scattered. Denominations and congregations deal with these polarities in different ways. What we know from experience is that being and doing constitute a polarity which cannot be broken. We must first be reconciled in order to be agents of reconciliation. But as we have learned, being reconciled is not something to be hidden or locked up in a safe place. In fact, for many, the act of being agents of reconciliation changes our lives. The same kind of dynamics relates to the church gathered and scattered. Over the past decades we have asked two questions. The first is: Were we able to go into the world to witness for justice and peace? The activist models of the church rightly reminded us that Christ is not only among the gathered but also in the world among those who suffer. Too often it appeared that the requirements of the church gathered tended to isolate the church from engagement with the world. The second is: Do our losses reflect a disregard for the church gathered? Did we assume the communities of faith were self-perpetuating? Recall the study that showed that much of the decline was due to the loss of our children after confirmation. Stated in another way, do churches lean toward the grace of forgiveness or the grace of transformative power? If the message and the weekly schedule only tends to speak of acceptance, then the idea that God expects something of us, or wills to change the world is probably not emphasized. (Try this simple test: when was the last time in worship it was made clear that God expects something of us?) Each of the six forms tries to deal with these issues in distinctive ways, and conversely fails in distinctive ways. What we need to do is see each form in its positive embodiment and compare positive to positive, rather than the best of one's own form against the worst of others.

In many ways we have lived in interesting times! Whereas the older generation began in a time where the differences between the six forms were strictly observed, we now experience a great deal of interaction between them, i.e., across denominational lines but also within congregations. I recall a lecture at Lancaster Seminary by a nationally-known peace activist, attended by Roman Catholics, Mennonites and centric Protestants. But there are still tensions and divisions between the six forms. Sometimes this emerges when a congregation discovers that a new pastor does not represent the dominant form present in the majority of members. At other times there are tensions in regional bodies and congregations when the different forms are set in opposition to one another, competing for time and program resources. Most of the time the rival groups are simply sub-groups within a congregation or denomination, which requires some means for bringing opposing groups together. In the UCC there occurs an unusual pattern where the national offices have been re-organized according to the model of love and justice, while regional conferences and congregations probably represent the traditional models of Word and faith and the gathered church, with various levels of interest in forms of love and justice and the liberationist model. As a result, the separation of local congregations from national offices reaches a high level, with no means to adjudicate conflict.

All this speaks to the underlying issue of the future of the centric Protestant tradition. Renewal of the tradition requires clarity over the form of the church. This need not mean uniformity or the domination of one form over others. It is also hard to imagine a community organized according to only one form. We have already demonstrated that congregations and denominations can affirm several forms. In many ways the openness to multiple forms can mean a fuller understanding of the gospel.

The purpose of this analysis of forms of the church has not been to outline a complete doctrine of the church. Rather it has been to emphasize two things: the first is that community is a defining mark of the church, though it takes different forms; the second is that in the process of recovery among centric Protestants we need clarity regarding which form or forms we affirm. The dominant form for this tradition has been that of Word and faith, wherein grace finds expression in Word and sacrament. That was very effective in focusing on the Word of promise which gives life in community and sets the vital center apart from worldly powers. It also contained within it a self-critical aspect regarding the church: the Word stands apart from and at times against the church, as well as among us and for us. In the present situation, surrounded by alternative religious groups and in the face of a hostile culture, it may serve us well to recover the full meaning of the church formed by Word and faith. By itself, however, it has not given enough attention to the themes in the other five forms. In this sense, it is enriched by incorporating aspects of these forms. This has in fact happened in our time, as evident by the openness to other forms. As a result, new things have emerged, even though it is not clear what the final result will be. Such choices enlarge the form of Word and faith. While there will be starts and stops, with considerable anxiety because we are in the middle and not at the end, such developments reflect a yearning for a more inclusive form of community reflecting the many forms of grace. The forms may be earthen vessels holding the treasure, but the earthen vessels are not irrelevant. They are the context for the way we envision our unity with God and one another. As such, they are signs of the eschatological goal for all creation.

D. Subversive Forces in Culture and the Church

If grace can be subverted by culture and the church, the same is true of community. Indeed, one aspect of the crisis is that too many see community as unnecessary baggage in their religious journey. We have also learned that the culture seldom nurtures communities of faith and that churches themselves can simply ignore or subvert the things which nurture community. As a result, community suffers. So it is that we need to name the problems.

The Cost of Individualism

American culture is constructed around the individual, considered to be the basic unit of society. This is also the case in religion: The free individual chooses to be religious, whether by oneself or in connection with religious communities. If there is to be a church, then it is defined as a voluntary association of like-minded individuals. American culture also contains a deeply rooted suspicion of institutions. Since the 1960s this has found expression in mistrust against all forms of government and corporations, as well as educational and religious organizations. The recent pandemic has seen open mistrust and opposition to science and national health organizations. We also need to admit that some of this suspicion regarding institutions is rooted in the Protestant insistence in the corruptibility of all people and institutions, even those dedicated to the highest values and goals. Such attitudes work against the support of religious communities. When institutions are regarded with suspicion and/or relegated to being merely the means for accomplishing certain ends, then communal images are not vital to the ways we think of religion.

Given these attitudes it is not a surprise that religious leaders—lay or ordained—prefer to speak of God's love but are hesitant to ask someone to join a church or give money. In the 1990s I attended a clergy gathering where a speaker, nationally known for inspiring clergy, declared that the gospel of Jesus Christ has nothing to do with the institutional church. Such a view not only encourages alienation between national bodies and local churches, but also disinterest in many of the things required for congregational life. Even among conservative Protestants, there is an unwillingness to identify with national denominations. My favorite example of independence nullifying the unity of Christians was a church sign in rural Pennsylvania which proclaimed: "Independent Fellowship Church." Once such suspicion of the church as an institution with connections to regional and national bodies occurs, the decline in numbers and dollars is inevitable. The problems faced by seminaries are directly related to decline in confidence in the church. If American religion established the practice that one can be religious without joining a church, now it appears that denominations are experimenting with the idea that churches don't need seminaries, i.e., one can have a denomination without the formation of leaders in a common ethos, faith and practice.

The freedom of the individual has also changed the way churches are governed. In my own denomination, the United Church of Christ, the

55

By-Laws of the church affirm the autonomy of each part of the church. This means, in spite of numerous declarations of being bound by covenantal relations, any part of the church may act independently of other parts. This appeal to autonomy goes back to the seventeenth and eighteenth centuries where Congregationalists sought freedom from the tyranny of kings and bishops. The problem is that in America today there are no longer kings or bishops to rule over us. But instead of developing a new form of connectionalism, the concern for religious freedom evolved in the nineteenth century into the principle of autonomy for each part of the church, with no means to resolve conflict. The result is church governance dominated by a culture of freedom. The irony of this is that the UCC has been strong on criticizing the culture for all manner of things which subvert the gospel. Yet in its basic organizational structure it mirrors American culture, affirming that we are bound to one another only if we agree. Lest you think this is a problem of one denomination, consider this: when I share my lament regarding the UCC principle of autonomy with Lutherans or Presbyterians, they indicate that the same problem exists in their denomination! It would appear that modern American culture has affected all branches of centric Protestantism. In one sense this should not surprise us, since Americans are hooked on liberty rather than equality.

The Elusive Search for Unity

One direct offshoot of the idea that the church is a voluntary association of like-minded people is the assumption that unity is based on commonality or agreement. The problem is this: If we do not start with the mandate contained in the peace of Christ, then the church will be defined—as it actually is—by nationality, race, class, gender, sexual orientation, political and economic preferences. Such a practice tends to nullify the radical transformation of our life by the gospel. Instead of breaking down barriers, the churches only re-enforce them. In this way the evangelical declarations of the gospel are denied or domesticated. Even the NT itself shows how difficult it is to follow the mandate of Christ: On the one hand, Paul rightly captured the new life in Christ as one where we are united without regard to gender, economic or ethnic status; on the other hand he was not able to withstand the pressures to revert to patriarchal practice. To this day, churches are divided on whether inclusion of women confers equality.

But the problem is not just at various levels of the church, where majority rule does not lead to agreement. Much of the centric movement of the past half-century has operated on the assumption that if we talk, study and pray, then over time we will reach agreement and that will be the basis for our unity. But having used this strategy unity still remains elusive.

What is needed is a completely new starting point. Unity is a gift of Christ: we are joined together by the will of God in spite of our weakness and sin, our disagreements, and our anger toward one another. Until we start with the recognition that unity is a gift of Christ in the face of the divisions of the world, we will find unity to be elusive. The unity embodied in the peace of Christ requires that we rethink the way we understand the church.

The Gospel without the Church or the Kingdom

The individualism of the culture has left its mark on the way the church itself frames the gospel. Hovering over all organized religion is popular American religion which defines God as the one who provides for our wants and needs. This popular religion is omnipresent by means of television and books, many falling in the category of self-help books. (Note that watching TV and reading are things one can do by oneself.) When God exists to further our ends, the basic question becomes whether God loves me. Conservatives are quick to affirm amazing grace, but tie the love of God to believing in a list of doctrines and moral positions, which are often quite restrictive. In response liberals are quick to object, arguing that God's love cannot be tied to institutional ends. Against a culture that is demanding and very legalistic, liberals affirm that God loves us unconditionally. In one sense this is prophetic and counter-cultural. But it also reflects the bias of the culture toward individualism. This proclamation of unconditional love seldom includes a call to be transformed by the grace of God or participate in the community of Christ. It thus becomes a proclamation of love disconnected from community and the coming of the kingdom of God. If one has heard the message, apparently you don't have to hear it again, nor is there a need to ask whether Jesus died on the cross for any purpose other than my needs. The question then is whether the gospel has been reduced to *cheap grace.*

There is no escape from this individually centered view of all things without introducing the image of a new covenant, the salvation of all people and the renewal of the creation, all set in an eschatological vision. If we are going to break with the individual-centered reading of the NT, then we will have to challenge the assumptions of popular religion in America. In the first and second centuries, Christians declared that Jesus is Lord as a counter-cultural affirmation against the claim that the emperor is Lord. Perhaps in our time such an affirmation of the Lordship of Christ will become the means to re-focus our faith, hope and love toward celebrating the community. Community is not something added on to the gospel, it is the gospel, i.e., the reconciliation of sinners to God in the new covenant of Christ. Moreover, that new community must be defined so that it includes not only human beings but also the restoration of the creation.

A Sacrament with Little Time for Community.

In Chapter 1 we discussed how Luther argued that the medieval Mass jeopardized the affirmation of grace. The continued use of the medieval framework by Protestants, however, has a second problem: it leaves no time for community. By this I refer to defining the Lord's Supper primarily in terms of the worthiness of members in their approach to the table and the grace of forgiveness to individuals. Bear in mind that most Protestant traditions developed services of preparation which focused on one's unworthiness and readiness to receive forgiveness in the Supper. Such a framework tends to exclude other images of salvation such as liberation from the powers of this world, be it sin, Satan and death, or reconciliation, or the renewal of the creation. This focus on sin and forgiveness of individuals is what I have referred to as the medieval framework and it reduces the Supper to a sacrament of penance. The emphasis falls upon sin, repentance, the recall of Jesus' death, our offerings to God—usually combined with the offering of Jesus himself to the Father—and our pleading for mercy. Consider the fact that in this framework, just before we receive the bread and wine, we sing the "Agnus Dei." In effect, before sharing bread and wine, we are still pleading for mercy with the outcome still in doubt. When bread and wine have been shared, a short prayer of thanksgiving is offered—so short that in one liturgy it takes thirty-five seconds. This ends the celebration of the Lord's Supper. A parting hymn is sung and the congregation is blessed and sent out. So we need to ask: Is this a celebration of the new covenant of Jesus Christ, rejoicing in the ways in which God is redeeming, reconciling and liberating the cosmos? Some will dismiss this question since most liturgies contain brief references to aspects of salvation other than forgiveness of sins. Perhaps we need to ask a different question to make the point: Why is the service so lacking in joy? There is so little joy because there is no time given to remember, celebrate, and proclaim the new life in Christ in the face of the coming kingdom of God. Since there is only time for sorrow and remorse for sin, there is no time for the community to celebrate its life in Christ. Once forgiven one is blessed and sent home, with the expectation that one will come back in a week and repeat the process, so that we never really move beyond the framework of sin and forgiveness to a celebration of the new reality God creates in Christ. Lest you think this is one writer's misreading of the liturgical tradition, consider Krister Stendal's critique of the Western restriction of the gospel to forgiveness of sin, or the critique offered by Eastern Orthodox in the name of a grand celebration of the re-demption of the whole world in Christ.[9]

We need to finish the reform of the sixteenth century, not only in terms of celebrating the fullness of salvation but also the celebration of the reality of new life in Christ in the community. This can easily be done without making the service longer by unifying the service of the Word and service of the table into one service. Many things which usually come in the service of the Word need to be placed in the celebration of the community after bread and wine are received: prayers of the people for the church and the world, the Lord's Prayer, the passing of the peace, joys and sorrows of the congregation, hymns of faith, hope and love, interspersed with passages of Scripture. The good news is that many churches have moved away from the theology of penal substitution. This opens the way for new perspectives. But one still wonders whether the anti-institutionalism of American reli-gion again shows its influence within church theology and practice. In spite of some dramatic and important changes, we are still left with the challenge of developing liturgies for the Word and table which affirm that the life of the community of Christ is a sign of the redemption Christ brings.

The subversions of the gospel illustrate that the church is broken and we can't fix it. We are so immersed in a culture of liberty and individualism that we resist the call of the gospel to be together in genuine community. Our history makes this clear, since we have divided the church by race and class, with women reduced to second class and persons of different sexual orientations only reluctantly allowed to join. What is needed is the trans-formation of our communities by the gospel of grace, allowing the Spirit to breathe life into our broken and incomplete forms. Those who wish to

9. Stendahl, "Introspective Conscience of the West." See also my discussion in *Gift and Promise*, chapters 3 and 5.

build churches on the basis of agreement with absolute doctrines and an infallible Bible are all around us, dominating the public religious culture. In such a situation only a Word of grace can overcome our resistance; only the peace of Christ can offer a new form of community.

3

Sin and Grace

CENTRIC PROTESTANTS AFFIRM A view of sin which may be called Christian realism. This sets them apart from both the religious left and right because it reclaims what is essential in the traditional view of sin, but not what might be called the negative baggage. Christian realism holds that specific bad acts proceed out of the way we think, love, and relate to others. In effect, the individual has been corrupted in multiple ways so that at the most basic level life is governed by self-interest. In this sense sin is a state of the heart and mind. The same is affirmed of society, i.e., what we refer to as social and historical networks have been similarly affected by self-interest and ill will. The problem is in us and our culture in a far more serious way than simply saying that we are prone to commit occasional bad actions. For this reason, realism refuses to exempt from the realm of sin certain people or institutions (e.g., churches claiming a special commission from Christ, or those born again, or gathered communities which have crossed over, or those claiming the purity of their love). As a result, realism leaves little room for claiming innocence. It places individual actions in the context of the person and the person in the context of the community, without relieving the individual of responsibility for such actions. For example, it makes no sense to explain terrible acts by appealing to the theory of the bad apple, i.e., that somehow the actions of an individual have nothing to do with the community so that while the individual is guilty of terrible acts, the larger society is completely innocent. Nor can acts of ill will or violence be blamed on the devil. What is surprising about the appeal to the devil is that it allows the perpetrator of bad acts to become a victim and claim innocence.

A. The Basic Idea

The twentieth-century revival of the Reformation theology of grace brought with it a revival of realism regarding the human condition. Two World Wars and a string of local wars, with genocide and racism, did indeed affect theology. In fact, it is impossible to understand the twentieth century theological revolution outside of that context. This revived the dependence on Paul, Augustine, Luther, and Calvin. However, this retrieval of the traditional view was modified and given a modern formulation. Yet it was also out of step with modern culture, which was usually outraged by the notion that sin could be passed from one generation to another. When the traditional view was translated into puritanical rules and regulations, it would often evoke laughter and flight. Everyone had their favorite instance of moral outrage at the very doctrine which is supposed to set the standard for what is morally acceptable. Consider the Roman Catholic woman who declared: "When the priest said that French kissing was a venial sin for boys and a mortal sin for girls, I said: 'I'm out of here.'"[1] All of this is to say that supporters of the traditional form of the doctrine are hard to find among Protestants. If liberals gave it up as an oppressive view of human nature and restrictive of freedom, many conservatives also lost interest in talking about individuals and social structures weighed down by the power of sin. In unpredictable ways, each side continued to use the word, but it was not clear what it meant. Each side carved out a safe zone for exemptions, where one could be fairly optimistic about individuals, the social status quo, or corporations and institutions which run things. Time and again religious traditions have been unwilling to admit that sin has consequences.

In such a context many cannot see what realism actually is without first clearing away the negative baggage. At some point we will have to do this. But I would prefer to begin with a process of retrieval to capture the essential idea in terms we can understand. If we can first do this, then we may have the will to discard what is unessential. In its simplest form Christian realism uses the word sin to acknowledge that something is seriously wrong regarding the human condition. We live in a world where acts of disobedience, selfishness, ill will, and betrayal disrupt human life. Such a

1. Seminary student at Lancaster Theological Seminary.

statement is corroborated by our personal experience as well as general reports in the news. Christians follow the Jewish perspective that sin is both a violation of moral standards but is also a religious problem. Thus the First Commandment in the Decalogue deals with love and loyalty towards God. In breaking relations with those near or far from us, we inevitably break relations with God.

In general all Christians acknowledge the existence of acts which are harmful to others and which break relations with God. The parting of ways comes in how we describe the origin of such bad acts and the consequences. Realism refuses to accept the idea that such acts are accidental or mistakes. There is a willfulness about sin which cannot be ignored without reducing it to triviality. But where did this willfulness come from? If it is something inherited at birth, that might suggest that sin is intrinsic to our nature. At this point realism proposes that sin must be interpreted as something *received* and as something *generated by each person*. We receive sin when we are born into a world already caught up in self-love, ill will and violence. We suffer the presence of those things which cause anxiety and separation from others and God. It is impossible for an individual not to experience the brokenness of the world. In this sense, sin is passed from one generation to another, though we need not think of this in biological terms, nor tie the transmission to sexual relations. But simultaneously, each person comes to accept such brokenness as part of life, and in his or her own way contributes to the brokenness of life by acts of selfishness and ill will. If the former affirms that human existence involves a tragic element not of our making, the latter affirms that each person recapitulates the experience of humankind and therefore we are partially responsible. We are not responsible for the sins of our parents, but we bear the consequences; we are responsible for our own sins and those around us inevitably bear the consequences. In this light, realism describes the consequences of sin as a *state of being* and as *a social-historical network of selfishness and violence.*

1. Sin as a State of Being

Realism assumes that persons have some form of continuing consciousness, or heart, mind and will, from which specific thoughts and actions proceed. For this reason religious education assumes persons may be formed in the ways of faith and moral practice. Our legal system assumes that persons intentionally commit crimes and are responsible for them. What is affirmed here is that persons may be formed in positive and negative ways. But how shall this be described? Is it a temporary problem, something we can correct, or a more serious impairment, like an addiction or permanent illness? Realism affirms that self-love and ill will have come to affect the very core of a person. In effect, it is a new state of being, though not our essential being nor one that may not be changed. When such deformation takes place, a person's being now is caught up in the tensions between positive habits of the heart and the vices and desires of the heart which lead to separation and division. Hence the preference for the images of *illness* and *bondage*, each implying the seriousness of the problem as well as a state of subjugation from which the person may not free himself or herself.

2. Sin as a Social or Historical Network

Sin as a state of being also relates to the world around us, as selfishness and ill will become incorporated into the social and historical networks of society. This leads to a circular movement: not only does society form the new born individual, but the individual thus formed claims ownership of the society and invents new ways to express selfishness and ill will. The fact is that the individual is born into families which are already marked by mistrust and self-love, into a world already at war, already committed to social-political values and ways of dealing with love, marriage, authority and division.[2]

What we have, then, is a general theory to explain the reality of sinful acts, resting on two assumptions: First, that being precedes doing, which means that bad acts arise from a person's heart and mind. Second, that the being of persons has been formed in negative ways by the social-historical networks embodying self-interest and ill will, which is to say that there is a solidarity of sin which affects the individual. As such, Christian realism is basically a reworking of the traditional view of sin, but without the negative baggage regarding sexual transmission. But it has had to face considerable resistance regarding the central idea. For this reason we need to consider the way realism relies on the Bible in the context of the twentieth century.

---

2. Not surprisingly, the debate over whether sin corrupts the very structures of society re-appears in the controversy over critical race theory. For Christian realism it is hard to avoid the conclusion that structural racism exists, since slavery and segregation were embodied in law, though this does not entail the further conclusion that such systems cannot be redeemed.

B. Realism and the Bible

1. Genesis 1–3

For the liberal tradition, Genesis represented mythological or legendary stories, which can no longer be taken seriously. For many religious conservatives they were actual accounts of creation and fall some five thousand years ago and must be accepted as authoritative. Any problems could be explained away. By appealing to these chapters, Christian realism proposed that there were more than these two options for reading the Bible. For realism, Genesis 1–3 affirmed something quite different from other origin stories from the ancient world. At the same time these chapters opposed the arrogance and pride of modern culture which assumed it could analyze and control everything, producing nothing but good. Genesis 1–3 shocks us by affirming:

a. All things are created by God's Word and Spirit and all things are good.

b. Sin is real and has altered human existence, but things were not meant to be this way. Genesis 1–2 envisions an original harmony between the man and the woman, between humanity and nature and humanity and God, whereas Genesis 3 reveals that something terrible has happened.

c. Genesis 3 takes up the burden of explaining how a good creation could become the world we now know. But unlike other origin stories in the ancient world, it refused to propose multiple gods representing good and evil, or warfare between gods, or a marriage of the gods. Nor will it affirm that whatever is wrong is intrinsic to the creation and therefore the world is beyond redemption. Genesis refuses to attempt a rational explanation, since it is hard to explain why a rational person would be dissatisfied with paradise. Instead, Genesis tells a story of human beings tempted by the desire to reach beyond their limits for something so attractive that they are willing to betray the compact with God. By telling a story of human temptation, the writers concede that all they can do is point to the strange workings of freedom and the human heart.

d. The key point in the story is the command not to eat of the tree of the knowledge of good and evil. This has often been misinterpreted either as a capricious limit on human freedom by a divine autocrat, or else it is seen as a limit on the full development of human potential. In a modern world where individuals wish to be free from autocratic power, be it parents, church or state, the stories arouse protests in the name of freedom and human growth. These interpretations suggest that independence from God is a prerequisite for human freedom. Both interpretations miss the point, which is the need to honor both human and divine identity. Human beings are made for life with one another and with God, but they are not God. Only God is God, i.e., possesses the knowledge of good and evil. When humans seek to possess godlike knowledge, they violate all relationships in the pretentious effort to be what they are not. The temptation, therefore, so subtly offered by the serpent, suggests that things go wrong when we aspire beyond the limits of our nature, thereby breaking trust with one another, with the creation itself and with God. When the man and woman aspire to be something they are not, they pose a threat to the other. As a result they cannot trust God or each other, but must hide and protect themselves. Nor can they be honest about what has happened, but blame it on one another or the serpent or even God. They are unable to take responsibility for their own action.

e. These passages suggest that the original intent has been violated and things have changed. The expulsion from the garden is but one symbol of this. Others are the fact that the man and woman no longer trust one another or God. Now that the bonds of love have been broken, when the misuse of one another is a possibility, they are afraid and must protect themselves from one another (i.e., put on clothes). In a world of ill will and selfishness, innocence is lost.

Realism concluded that the liberal confidence in the rational person, capable of freeing oneself from ignorance, hatred and ancient rivalries, could not explain the horrors of the twentieth century. It could not explain all that had happened by categories of accident, limited knowledge or bad planning. Racism, anti-Semitism and military aggression were intentional devices of human minds and hearts, based on self-interest and ill will. What was needed was to recognize the reality of these things and that they are in us and that we are part of the problem. In other words, realism thought that Genesis 1–3 was more honest about the human condition than the lofty claims of liberalism.

The Prophetic Perspective

Christian realism also relied on major themes in the prophetic tradition. First, in the prophets sin is viewed from a theological perspective: it is fundamentally a violation of the relation between Israel and God. Second, Israel's obligation to God is understood in covenantal terms: God is the God who brought Israel out of bondage and created the covenant of Moses. To be sure there are classic episodes involving a prophet and a major figure (e.g., Nathan and David). But the prophetic rage is most often directed at Israel itself. Israel has forgotten what God has done. As a result Israel has lost its way and does not know who it is. Third, God's opposition to sin is expressed in two frightening responses: judgment and wrath. It is the people who have become impure, as if changed by an infection which spreads and can only get worse. So God will judge and destroy the very people God has created. But in a most surprising way, judgment and wrath are not the last word. No matter how bad things seem, the prophetic vision holds out the hope that God will redeem Israel. This redemption will involve a return or turning back to the God of the patriarchs and Moses as well as a restoration of the land. Like Deuteronomy, where the covenant is seen in terms of love of God and neighbor, redemption will involve a cleansing or renewal of hearts and minds and a reaffirmation of faith.

These themes were important for realism in its attempt to undercut the liberal tendency to reduce religion to ethics and disconnect the individual believer from the community. To be sure, the prophets had little regard for religious practices as a substitute for just dealings in the life of the community. But now the prophets spoke for the religion of the covenant, where love of God meant love of widows and orphans. Just as important, the prophetic critique was all encompassing. It held the society to account as well as the individual. There could be no separation of private and public life. Moreover, the solution is not going to be people pulling themselves up by their bootstraps but a willingness to accept the judgment of God and turn (returning by repentance) to the God of the covenant. As Joel 2:13 declares: "Rend your hearts and not your garments."

3. The New Testament

From the perspective of a rational and well-ordered world, where one may expect good will to move society toward positive goals and where individuals can control their lives and overcome obstacles, the NT is a strange document. The world is run by oppressive tyrants, acquisition of wealth and power dominate human relations, and people fear demonic forces and death. The religious tradition is divided into factions, with alliances with those in political power while the poor are left to suffer their fate. Even the devout are not sure what is required and are tempted to tie their hearts to things other than God. The basic story is about the tensions between the rule of God and the forces of this world, between choosing God verses saving oneself according to worldly wisdom. It portrays a chosen one whose very presence excites fear and the killing of the innocent, divides families, and arouses such opposition that he is arrested and crucified, only to be raised as Lord to rule over all the powers of this world until God will unite all things in him in the end time.

In the twentieth century, Christian realism found this strange world of the NT, with its language of tension, violence and divine intervention, to be a more accurate description of the human condition than that of the older liberal and Pelagian narratives. There was no argument about people being overcome by self-interest, fear or greed—these things were simply there. One did not have to argue that society and political power could be oppressive—one only needed to look at the world. Nor was there any hesitation to admit that we were part of the problem. Why else would Jesus begin by announcing the coming of the rule of God and immediately call for repentance? Why would Paul speak of the solidarity of all people in the grip of sin, leading to the need for dying to the old and rising to the new? And then there is John, suggesting that we must be born again, a figurative image parallel to Paul's insistence that we must have the mind of Christ (in contrast to our old mind) and live in the power of Christ and the Spirit.[3]

All of this is to say that realism drew its perspective out of the Bible. It did not impose a preferred political agenda on the Bible. What caught the eyes of advocates of realism was the emphasis on the solidarity of all people in sin and its consequences, as well as the divine initiative which liberates and reconciles. Amid the terrors of the times, realism could connect powerful images from Genesis and the prophets with the NT to interpret in new ways the world as it is and the world as God would have it be.

---

3. Writing this in the spring of 2022 one wonders whether the devastation of Ukraine and the turmoil in the American political system constitutes an unveiling of the idols similar to that of the two World Wars and the genocide against Jews in the first half of the twentieth century.

C. Realism and Alternatives from the Ancient World

In an unexpected way, the doctrine of sin is the keystone holding its coun-
terparts together. If you remove it, the others collapse. The reason for this
is quite simple. Realism affirms the reality of sin and evil, but also that they
constitute a fall from the original goodness of creation. If you take away
these affirmations, then one is faced with problems: on the one hand, if sin
and evil are intrinsic to the creation, then you have destroyed the view of
one God and the goodness of creation. On the other hand, if one denies
the reality of sin and evil, one diverges from the confession that God in
Christ has redeemed the world and that Jesus is more than a moral teacher.
Against such possibilities, the doctrine of sin holds creation and redemption together: something has gone seriously wrong, corrupting the individual and society, but it arises within the world.

Consider several major alternatives from the ancient world as a way of
emphasizing the distinctive nature of the biblical view of sin.

1. Cosmic dualism (e.g., Manichaeism) proposes that good and evil arise
from the fact that the world is created by more than one deity. In the
second century Marcion proposed that Christians incorporate a form
of dualism into the faith, separating the creator God of Genesis from
the redemptive God of Jesus Christ. This would have meant a rejection of the OT and acceptance of polytheism.

2. Gnosticism was intentionally polytheistic and drew on the distinction
between the spiritual and physical. The human spirit was imprisoned
in the world of physical matter, lost in darkness. Salvation was possible, however, by the intervention of a savior from the realm of Spirit
and light, who comes into the world with the knowledge (i.e., gnosis)
on how we can be freed to heavenly realms. On these terms, Jesus
could easily be presented as a heavenly redeemer, but this too was
rejected because of its polytheism and its denigration of physical matter. Note that in rejecting both Marcion and Gnosticism, Christians
deliberately chose to stay within the general framework of Jewish
thinking, i.e., there is one God, the world is good, if there are problems
they originate within this world and salvation is not an escape from or
denial of this world.

3. Demonization is like dualism, though it selectively designates certain
portions of the creation as evil. This allows for a clear separation of

good and evil. If the American Shakers give us a fanciful example (i.e., sin was so embodied in sex that they became celibate), more serious examples of demonization occurred in the twentieth century in terms of genocide. Any time a person, or group or thing is declared to be evil and the source of the problem, you have demonization which inevitably leads to proposals to remove such evil.

Christian opposition to these ancient alternatives finds expression in the Nicene Creed. By insisting on the incarnation of the divine Word, the Nicene Creed affirmed the Christian framework: one God, a good creation, the reality of sin, and the possibility of salvation in this world by the presence of God's Word and Spirit. Indeed, one can see a hint of the dualism of infinite and finite, spirit and matter in the Arian insistence that the divine, heavenly Word could not be the same as the Word in Jesus Christ. Most important, the view of sin contained in this brief credo affirms that sinners can be redeemed. The fall is not permanent; the fallen can be raised to new life. In contrast to demonization, they do not have to be isolated or destroyed. But having set forth how Christian faith resists the ancient alternatives, we now need to take up the disturbing question: Why is Christian history filled with elements suggestive of these alternatives? Consider the following:

1. Monasticism and religious orders hold up the ideal of life dedicated to holiness and union with God, but they also do this at the expense of the removal of members from family, marriage and the world.

2. In many instances, sexuality has been denigrated or even demonized:

   - Religious orders practice celibacy, whereas the non-celibate laity represent a lower level of faithfulness.

   - For centuries the transmission of sin has been connected to procreation.

   - To maintain the sinlessness of Jesus some Christians appeal to the virgin birth and the immaculate conception of Mary.

   - At times the emphasis on salvation as passage to heaven overwhelms the affirmation of redemption for life on earth. Religion takes on a spiritual form separate from life on earth.

   - Demonization has been prevalent throughout Christian history, as a means of separating good from evil, as well as justifying violence.

- The ecological crisis reveals the extent to which human beings have set themselves apart from nature: either we have declared war on nature or simply reduced it to a neutral state, allowing us to do what we want with it. While this may not be full blown Manichaeism, it does mean that nature has no value unless we grant it—a view quite unbiblical.

3. Finally, the tendency to spiritualize Christian faith, i.e., setting the spiritual life apart from life on earth suggests the influence of the ancient alternatives. In one form, religious life is defined in terms of spiritual matters set apart from worldly affairs. The goal of heaven far outweighs any goals for the transformation of the earth. In another form, the realm of spiritual values is separated from the earth itself. We no longer live in and with nature. This becomes a major issue in a time of environmental crisis: is our disregard for nature rooted in the separation of the spiritual world of values from the natural order? Compare the excellent work of H. Paul Santmire regarding the separation of nature from the spiritual world of religion in *The Travail of Nature*.[4]

The question becomes: why are there such strong tendencies toward the dualism of spirit/matter in Christian faith? The affirmations of one God, a good creation, sin and grace are supposed to defend against these ideas. Yet here we are still struggling with how to speak of sin without lapsing into the dualism of good and evil, spirit and matter, and demonization. To be sure, some will say that the problem is in the eye of the beholder. Roman Catholics will object to the suggestion that monasticism and celibacy denigrate the creation. Still others will not want to deal with the negative images of sexuality in religion and the culture. Others will object that the environmental crisis reveals a denial of the goodness of creation. But can we appreciate the genius of Christian realism, based on Genesis 1–3, without turning a critical eye on the ways we compromise it?

D. The Pelagian Alternative

There is another view from the ancient world which challenges the doctrine of sin, only this time it is internal to faith. This is the Pelagian alternative. If Christian realism judges the problem facing us as *very bad*, the Pelagian alternative treats the problem as *not so bad*. Indeed, this may be its appeal.

4. Santmire, *Travil.*

While it has officially been stamped as heretical, it has resurfaced in every age and currently is a mainstay of much of American religion.

It should be noted that this view arises out of a devout moral concern. Both Judaism and Christianity affirm that the holy God wills God's people to be holy. When a contemporary of Augustine thought about this, he concluded that God would not command us to do the good if we were unable to do it. In that moment, Pelagius moved away from Augustine by assuming that whatever has gone before is not so bad as to disable or impair our ability to do the good. Pelagius rejected the two great images used to describe sin (sickness and bondage) to affirm that while sin exists, we still retain the freedom, reason and a purity of heart to do God's will. Therefore we can lead a moral life. Failures must be treated with remorse and renewed discipline. But the radical idea that we are so immersed in our sinful ways that we can only be saved by grace is excessive. We may need help and encouragement, but not new birth or transformation.

Pelagius's views were rejected at the Council of Carthage in 418, but they lived on in a variety of forms, for example, confidence in reason, human potential and self-reform. Luther considered many of the religious practices of his time to be immersed in a Pelagian mindset: people were encouraged to prepare themselves for receiving grace, make offerings and do good works (e.g, indulgences) to assure their salvation. Even the Lord's Supper was perceived as our action toward God as a means to receive grace. To oppose this view, Luther took refuge in Paul and Augustine, and of course key sayings in the gospels. The first thesis in the *Ninety Five* declared that repentance was a life-long process.[5] But like Augustine, Luther did not resolve the problem. In America Pelagian optimism is very much a part of the culture and runs parallel to the rationalism of the eighteenth century and liberal religion. But it also appears unexpectedly in popular American religion, which in language and substance is supposed to be quite conservative.

E. Christian Realism in America

1. The Enlightenment and the American Liberal Tradition

The Enlightenment proposed a new starting point for critical thinking, religion and political thought, namely the individual freed from the restrictions

---

5. Luther, *Ninety-Five Theses*, x.

of tradition, state and church. Instead of accepting the received traditions controlled by kings and bishops, the individual could access truth by direct appeal to reason. For religion the consequences were enormous. The rational individual was freed from adopting traditional views and able to interpret Scripture on one's own. Ideas about sin as something received or as a social-historical network could be set aside. The individual possessed the capacity to liberate oneself from either societal or self-imposed bondage. One therefore arrived at the surprising conclusion of innocence. If one has not personally engaged in all manner of evil deeds, even those done on our behalf, then one is freed from any responsibility for them.

By the beginning of the twentieth century, American liberalism displayed the confidence of both the Enlightenment and the Pelagian tradition. New knowledge, science and technology were changing the world, resulting in a general confidence and claims to innocence. When the failures of society were lifted up, it was assumed that reason, morality, education and rational planning could mitigate these negative forces.

World War I changed all of that—at least temporarily. In 1914, political, cultural and religious leaders knew that the chief parties were planning for war but no one—not even royal households connected by blood—could stop it. Then there was the duration of the war, with unspeakable brutality and casualties. The final nightmare was that there was no way to end it, leaving it to drag on for years with a conclusion so flawed it would be blamed for yet another war.

For many religious liberals, the war meant an end to the idea that the world would be progressively changed by reason, religion and the ethics of love. In 1932 Reinhold Niebuhr proposed in *Moral Man and Immoral Society*, a new set of categories to describe social conflict. In effect, religion, reason, morality failed to recognize that self-interest and ill will corrupted the individual, and even more so, the society. While the principle of love was indeed the highest moral standard, in most cases social justice could only be achieved by the use of coercive power. Having shocked the liberal world by a defense of violent coercion in certain circumstances, he then made the case for non-violent coercion as a preferred strategy on moral and strategic grounds.[6]

---

6. Regarding the limits of reason and religion, cf. Reinhold Niebuhr, *Moral Man and Immoral Society*, ch. I-VI; regarding the need for coercion in the cause of justice and the superiority of non-violent coercion, cf. ch. VII-X.

What emerged in Europe and America was a theological revival often called neo-orthodox because it was so dependent on the Reformers, creeds and biblical theology. By reintroducing the language of the Bible, it produced Christian realism—a revised version of the Pauline and Augustinian view of sin. Most important was the use of the Bible. Instead of recoiling from the strangeness of the Bible, realism embraced it. It found the language of disobedience, betrayal, and violence to be a more accurate description of the human condition than the older liberal views. The Bible did not hide from the fact that people were overcome by self-interest, fear or greed, or that society and political power could be oppressive. Nor was there any hesitation to admit that we were part of the problem. Why else would Jesus' announcement of the rule of God include a call for repentance? Paul did not hesitate to speak of the solidarity of all people in the grip of sin, leading to the need for dying to the old and rising to the new? And then there is John, suggesting that we must be born again, a figurative image parallel to Paul's insistence that we must have the mind of Christ and live in the power of Christ and the Spirit.

All this is not to say that everything in the NT was simple and clear. There were still many issues unresolved, such as the meaning of demon possession, apocalyptic sayings, as well as the status of women, slaves and outcasts. But what was decisive was the realistic view of sin regarding individuals and society as well as the divine initiative which liberates and reconciles. Amid the terrors of the times, realism could connect powerful images from Genesis and the prophets with the NT to interpret the world.

2. Realism between Liberals and Religious Conservatives

In general discussions, centric Protestants are usually described as liberals, which may explain why conservative Protestants are often so opposed to them. In many ways this association is warranted. Centric Protestants are committed to democratic values, endorse public education, higher education and display a high regard for science and history. They have little patience for attempts to ignore new knowledge or to deny portions of American history, generate *alternative facts*, or ban books because they make us uncomfortable. In the culture wars, when faced with issues regarding freedom, equality, or the environment, they usually side with the liberal positions.

At the same time there are serious issues which separate centric Protestants from liberal views and practices. For one thing, liberal culture has adopted a general pragmatic and secular perspective, which leaves little room for religion. This tends to confine religion to the private realm of the personal or subjective, in the hope of opening the way for a value-free public life based on technological and monetary goals. In the end religion is pushed to the edges.[7] For example, over three generations many colleges founded by churches have made the study of religion and ethics optional, which is the case at state sponsored institutions. It is almost as if we decided that bright people do not need to know anything about religion or ethics. This creates an educated public which knows about science, math, business, finance, psychology and politics, but very little about Jewish, Christian or Muslim traditions—the very traditions at the heart of recent wars. In a related way, when foreign policy decisions are made entirely on the basis of political, economic and military self-interest, it is not surprising that small minority groups like the Kurds receive little attention in settlements in the Middle East.

A second point of tension is that the individualism of liberal culture too often prevents an embrace of community, as religion and even Jesus are separated from the church.

Perhaps the most serious point of contention is the liberal confidence in human reason and the capacity to reform oneself, in both the practice of religion or the general approach to issues in the culture. Naïve optimism appears to rule the day. For example, in recent years we find political leaders surprised that creative and bright people might use the internet for negative purposes or excessive monetary gain. Neither liberals nor conservatives seem to be working with a sense of the corruptibility of all things. Much of this goes back to the tendency of liberals to define freedom in terms of self-actualization and self-expression, whereas conservatives see freedom as a defense of conservative values and the social status quo. When dealing with oppressive practices on a social scale toward women or minorities, liberals join in protesting for justice. But they also tend to carve out exemptions from critical analysis in the realm of personal relations such as love, marriage or family, even though such practices might be harmful to women and children.

Given these factors, the relation of centric Protestants to liberal culture is a delicate balance, with major concerns separating the two. If liberals see Christian realists still hanging on to a long list of dubious religious ideas, realists see liberals as unable to accept a radical appraisal of the human

7. Stephen L. Carter, *Culture of Disbelief*, 1–66.

condition. What we have then, much to the frustration of many, is that centric Protestants find themselves *between* liberals and conservatives: sometimes they rely on one side or the other, while unable to fully embrace either.

In the first half of the twentieth century, conservative Protestants played defense, resisting the influence of modern science and liberal culture in the attempt to uphold orthodox doctrines and/or the fundamentals of the faith. Many chose to make an inerrant Bible a line of defense. By the 1960s, however, things had changed. As centric Protestants began the long process of decline, conservatives grew stronger in numbers and in confidence. Billy Graham emerged as the most popular preacher in America and chaplain to conservative politicians. While he officially still held the line on a literal reading of the Bible, his operational message was more of grace rather than the law. The polarization between liberals and conservatives in the culture war found conservative Protestants joining forces with political conservatives over Vietnam, civil rights, women's rights, abortion, gay rights and a defense of the status quo.

But the emergence of conservatives as the dominant Protestant group brought an unusual development relating to the doctrine of sin. This was the movement away from the traditional view, in favor of the individualism, optimism and innocence of America in general. It is not at all clear how to explain this. One might attribute it to tendencies in the free church tradition where believers cross over to a higher state. Or it might be seen as a semi-Pelagian reading of faith: by belief in Jesus and pledging to live a new life one is elevated to innocence. One might even interpret it as political expediency, as religious conservatives adapt the message to the political agenda. In some cases it reflected a kind of popular religion wedded to traditional faith, as in Peale, Schuler and Osteen. Whatever one proposes will, however, be roundly criticized because conservative Protestants consist of so many different traditions.[8] There will be differences on these issues between orthodox Lutherans and Reformed, Mennonites and Southern Baptists. At this point it is not necessary to explain why this movement away from the traditional view of sin happened, but simply to name it as the new reality held by much of conservative Protestantism.

The point, then, is that centric Protestants find themselves responding to conservatives who appear to have basically rejected the main tenants of realism. By claiming that faith in Christ confers innocence and freedom from the corruptions of heart, mind and will, some conservatives appear to

8. Cf. the definition of conservative Protestants in the introduction.

deny that sin is a state of being generated by fallen humanity. If we are innocent, because we ourselves have not committed certain crimes, then the basic idea that sin is something received which corrupts us appears to be denied. On such terms the idea of being born again implies that Christians no longer experience the struggle of sin and grace, the old and the new. Such a position creates two difficulties.

One is the inability to explain the presence of sin among Christians. Now of course, one can argue that people who commit bad acts are not Christians. But there are limits to solving the problems by redefining terms. In general, three explanations are offered: One is that a person comes under bad influences, though there is little discussion where such influences come from or why a Christian is tempted by such. A second is to appeal to the theory of the *bad apple*. This acknowledges the reality of the sin but seeks to disassociate the perpetrator from those around him or her. But in so many situations involving alcohol, sex, greed or hate crimes, it is very difficult to isolate the offender from the larger community. A third is to blame it on the devil. This again appeals to a cause outside of us, even to the point of making the offender a victim rather than morally responsible. It is hard to avoid the conclusion that all of these explanations are attempts to cover up what is the reality of the human condition.

The second difficulty is that the claim to innocence makes believers extremely vulnerable. If faith expects perfection, then anything less jeopardizes the primary claim that we are saved and bound for heaven's rewards. This then opens the door to a new legalism where one must maintain innocence, but also the need to defend oneself against any charge. If going to heaven requires innocence, how can one possibly admit any faults, such as structural racism? One can only wonder whether the vehement negative reaction to any discussion of racism is triggered by such a mindset: there is no way we can admit to what happened in the history of slavery, segregation and current practices since that would mean we are not good—and only good people go to heaven.[9]

The emerging view of sin among much of conservative religion also involves the denial that sin exists in the world as social-historical networks, taking form in the very structure and practices of society as well as corrupting the hearts and minds of individuals. There probably are no official

---

9. From this perspective one can imagine the shock which occurred—not just the laughter—when President Jimmy Carter acknowledged his discomfort with Matt 5:27–28.

documents by church bodies declaring such a position, but it becomes evident in the long history of the culture wars. It would appear that faith in Jesus Christ brings an obligation to adhere not only to certain personal standards but to defend the status quo. This appears to be happening not only by denying that certain things happened in American history but also refusing to talk about them.[10]

It is quite possible that some will say that many conservative Protestants don't agree with centric Protestants because they never adopted the Reformers' view of justification by grace. In line with this approach one might also see the tendencies toward perfection and innocence as rooted in the free church claim to gather the saints in the beloved community. By contrast, some will rightly object that all conservative Protestants cannot be lumped together and deny that the doctrine of sin has been compromised. To be sure, not all have embraced a Pelagian turn. The presence of vigorous theological discussion among confessional churches, Evangelicals, Anabaptists and other conservative Protestants makes this clear. But that still leaves us asking how the majority of conservative Protestants could end up opposed to Christian realism and link arms with conservative political social policies. However one explains the development among conservative Protestants, the fact is that centric Protestants find themselves viewing the doctrine of sin in very different terms than liberals or conservatives.

F. Sin and Grace

To complete the discussion of the doctrine of sin, we need to consider the connection between sin and grace. How does grace relate to and transform human beings caught in a web of self-interest, where hearts and minds have been turned away from God? The good news begins with a gracious intervention which changes the options before us. One new option is a call to repentance, based on God's vindication of the crucified, culminating in a new covenant on earth. It is a process of transformation of sinners, but not a gathering of perfect people who save themselves.

---

10. A great debate occurred when Harper Lee's other book was published (cf. *Go Set a Watchman*), since it portrayed Atticus Finch as a defender of the status quo rather than as the defender of justice in *To Kill a Mockingbird*. But the two portraits are consistent: in one he is an honest lawyer defending a man falsely accused; in the other he will not support social reforms of society, especially if they come from Northerners in Washington.

In Paul this plays out in the affirmation of solidarity of all people in sin as well as the new solidarity of believers in Christ. At this point realism presents us with a paradox: we still participate in sin and its consequences in terms of a fallen world, but our deformation is not intrinsic to our nature. Thus the good news is that Christ incorporates sinners into new life. We are therefore sinful and redeemed at one and the same time. The world is not divided between good and bad people, but sinners who by grace participate in new life and sinners who are still outside the community of new life—a theme on which Luther will build. By grace sinners are incorporated into Christ and receive the gifts of freedom, joy and peace with God, but not perfection in this life. This means that those in Christ confess that they are forgiven, are welcomed into the community as sons and daughters, are freed from the judgment of God even though they still bear the marks of life dominated by sin. The final word is not that we live in separation from God, constantly humiliated by our sin, but are brothers and sisters in Christ. If it were not so, there would be no peace or joy.

Justification by grace received by faith opposes the Pelagian alternative in two senses: first by incorporating realism into its understanding of the human condition and by understanding salvation as a gift of grace rather than our work. Since the struggle of sin and grace continues in our lives, there is no possibility of claiming innocence. If there is any security in this paradox, it is relying on the grace of God in Christ, who died for us. This is always the sticking point for various forms of Pelagianism. In the Roman Catholic form, there is still the claim that we possess the capacity to turn toward God, or turn with the assistance of grace. Sin is sorted out in terms of major and minor sins, with a sacramental system that parcels out forgiveness in relation to a scale of offenses. Even the Lord's Supper is seen as our work toward pleasing God. Thus the full force of realism and of grace is muted. Among conservative Protestants, there can be a grand bargain whereby our decision for Christ leads to sharing of Christ's gifts and the claim to innocence. But the claim to innocence is impossible to maintain. This produces the dilemma: if one claims innocence, one is vulnerable to a charge of hypocrisy; if one admits one participates in the solidarity of sin, one faces condemnation because salvation is only for the innocent. By contrast, the paradox of grace is precisely that only grace allows us to repent and admit the evils we do as well as the evils done on our behalf.

A Last Word: The Negative Language
Associated with Original Sin

At the start of the chapter I preferred to begin with a positive definition of Christian realism than attempt to clear away all the negative baggage related to the traditional doctrine. It is difficult to mention criginal sin without someone objecting to the idea of sin and guilt inherited by new born infants. Then there is, as mentioned, all the negative baggage about human sexuality and the issues related to celibacy. While there may be reasons for affirming the virgin birth, the idea that it is needed, along with Mary's immaculate conception, to defend the sinlessness of Jesus, is one more unnecessary burden. The NT makes clear that there are other ways of affirming Jesus' sinlessness.

In this chapter a case for Christian realism has been presented without depending on any of these burdens associated with the traditional doctrine of sin. The modern social sciences have given us more than enough ways to explain how life turned in on itself can result in habits and patterns of behavior, even addictions, which are incorporated into the larger society and affect new generations. The Bible is quite perceptive regarding the strange workings of love and the human heart. There are also ample theological and moral writings which explore the corruptibility of reason.

Yet opposition to realism persists, in spite of family tragedies or local and world events. In a strange way one might well wonder how a culture so committed to optimism, reason and innocence could spend so much time watching the news, reading newspapers, literature or the extensive literature of mystery stories, which tend to make the case for moral realism. Even the announcers of tennis matches use the phrase "We see with our hearts," to explain why players and fans disagree with calls. It may be inevitable that the case for realism will always have to be made against strong opposition.

4

Authority

Schaff's Proposal

IN 1845 PHILIP SCHAFF proposed in *The Principle of Protestantism* that justification by grace and Scripture, taken together, constituted the principle of authority for the Reformers.[1] Schaff's presentation was a tour de force. By using the symbols *sola gratia* and *sola scriptura*, he captured the genius of the Reformers and framed the discussion of authority. The principles functioned as positive values guiding faith and practice. At the same time he could use them as critical tools against the traditional adversary (Roman Catholics) and the new nineteenth century challenges from rationalism and sectarianism in America. Time and again Protestants have looked to these principles for inspiration. They are embedded in our confessional documents, in the way we worship and preach, and many of us carry them in our hearts. But the proposal raises several questions.

The Order of the Two Parts

Why did Schaff begin with the material principle of grace followed by the formal principle of scripture? Would it not have been more logical to begin with the formal principle, since it is more general? If used first, it would signal to the reader that the Reformers were faced with multiple sources

1. Schaff, *Principle*, 75–124.

of authority, which too often conflicted. There was of course Scripture, but also creeds, decisions of councils, theological traditions, the practice of the church over centuries, and the power of bishops. By claiming Scripture, the Reformers were setting it opposition to the other authorities and elevating Scripture to be the primary authority. If one began with Scripture, one could then affirm grace as the primary message of Scripture.

But that was not how Schaff saw things and definitely not how he presented them. He began with the principle of grace—the central message of the gospel. However, this by itself could not settle things, since the tradition and church authorities interpreted grace in different ways. Something was needed to nullify appeals to these other interpretations of grace and this was found in the appeal to Scripture. Scripture was now used as a defensive strategy, setting a limit on what was acceptable and not acceptable. This allows us to see things in a new way. If Schaff is correct, Luther did not begin one day with the declaration that everything had to be according to Scripture. He began with grace and used *sola scriptura* to hold off the attacks from tradition and church authorities. Schaff's order of the principles is supported by the historical record. Luther had been reading Scripture for years, but it was not until his rediscovery of grace in Romans that things exploded. One might also ask a hypothetical question: What if Luther rediscovered grace while studying the tradition, say for example, in Augustine rather than Paul? That would lead to just one more debate *between* the traditions, going nowhere unless bishops sided with him—which was fairly obviously not going to happen. This suggests that one might argue that Luther's call to reform would go nowhere unless he coupled it with something that would withstand the authority of tradition and the church. It also explains why, when Luther refers to the authority of Scripture, it is not to every word of the Bible but to the Word of God, which is the Word of promise or grace.[2] From this perspective, grace and Scripture do indeed form a necessary polarity: grace is the central theme but must be interpreted by Scripture; Scripture is the Word of God but given the size of Scripture there must be a standard for unlocking its central message, namely grace. The implications of this should not be overlooked: grace is the starting point; Scripture is the great shield of faith, understood as the Word of God revealed in the grace of Jesus Christ.

---

2. When Luther speaks of the Commandments or the sacraments, he constantly refers to the Word of God, which is a Word of grace. Cf. *Large Catechism*, 4, 21–22, 82–86.

One or Many Authorities?

A second perplexing issue is the fact that Schaff speaks of the Protestant principle (singular) when in fact he is compelled to subdivide it into two parts: grace and Scripture. There is good reason for this twofold formulation, as evidence by the way each part is essential in understanding the other. But what if this formulation points to a much larger issue: while we may indeed claim a single center of authority, we still function with many other centers of authority. Schaff appears to open the door to this possibility by a twofold principle. Neither grace nor scripture by itself captures the point of the Reformation. A similar point is affirmed by the Methodist quadrilateral: Scripture, tradition, reason and experience. Such a development is striking, simply because it acknowledges that we do in fact function with more than Scripture. If we examine changes in faith and practice we find that they often involved the need to adjudicate tensions between what is considered primary and secondary standards, such as tradition, creeds, landmark decisions, communal life, culture and experience. In one sense the Roman Catholics have recognized this when they hold that it is task of the community (i.e., bishops and tradition) to adjudicate the tensions between multiple centers of authority.

Perhaps the resistance to recognizing a more dynamic and complex understanding of authority comes from a fear that we will appear to be disloyal to what we claim to be primary, or that we have capitulated to the pressures of culture. The two great conservative traditions surrounding centric Protestants—Roman Catholics and conservative Protestants—are quick to denounce any changes in what is considered the orthodox faith and practice. Such an approach assumes an absolutely fixed standard, no matter how much the world changes. Decisions are simply a matter of looking up traditional answers and requiring compliance. Moreover, it is further assumed that any change is the beginning of the end, since the whole system rests on the idea of an unchangeable standard.

Centric Protestants have not taken such a view of authority. The reason for this is that from the beginning attempts to define what is authoritative point to God and God's relation to us. We see this is Schaff's conclusion that justification by grace is the primary principle, or in Luther's preference for speaking of the Word of promise. This is quite different from claiming a set tradition or even every word of the Bible as inerrant, because it allows one to affirm that the Word always appears in this world of change and conflict. Since it is a living Word of promise, it is able to deal with the actual situation in time and space, rather than impose one rule on all times and places. It is like the changing scenes in the gospels, where a different set of people, with new questions and challenges, require new words of Jesus. It is the same Word, but always a Word in context.

In this light it is possible and even necessary to posit a primary authority but also recognize that we function with multiple loyalties of lesser degree. In some instances these other loyalties impinge on us in ways which we did not expect or even like, but over time they must be incorporated into faith and practice. For example, Christians did not ask for the older cosmology to be shattered by the Copernican revolution. But it happened and in coming to terms with it we discovered that the primary norm did not change though we may think about it in new ways. This did not mean that science is now the primary norm, but it does mean that the primary norm of grace/Scripture must recognize other norms which impinge upon us. In this light, the proposal regarding authority in this chapter will posit a primary authority but also recognize how it is surrounded by other centers of authority. This recognizes that specific issues may require a different cluster of secondary authorities.

Clarifications

What is striking about Schaff's work is that he tells us quite clearly that it is dated.[3] He saw that in America, Roman Catholics were no longer the greatest challenge. Rationalism, revivalism and independent sects now posed what Schaff (and Nevin) called the church question: Do individual believers need the church, sacraments, creeds and traditions to form faith and practice? That is a very different question than the primary issue facing Luther. But we now live in the twenty-first century where new challenges have presented themselves as we attempt to determine the meaning of grace and Scripture in the current crisis.

Sola Gratia

Schaff rightly perceived that anyone claiming Scripture needed to declare what was the operative principle for interpreting it. He concluded that for the Reformers grace was the key to Scriptures. But this leaves open several

---

3. Schaff, *Principle*, 264–68.

issues. At the start there is the relation of justification to sanctification, an issue which separated many Protestants. Then there is the matter of the fullness of grace: besides forgiveness of sins (justification) there are other forms of saving power. How does forgiveness of sins relate to images of reconciliation, liberation from the powers of sin, death and the devil, the true knowledge of God as well as the renewal of the earth? Can justification by grace be re-fined so as to develop a more inclusive view of salvation?

Finally and much harder to achieve will be the task of defining grace as a counter balance against the rampant individualism of American religion. In our liturgies and preaching, justification by grace has been understood as a message directed toward individuals in their relation to God. In what I call "popular American religion," whatever the NT intends is translated in a religion *all about me*. In many respects this reveals the American preference for liberty rather than equality. For centuries American churches chose to co-exist with a culture which incorporated slavery and segregation, as well as the subordination of women. This required open declarations of inequality but also various attempts to rationalize such divisions in the body of Christ. Even Schaff underestimated the horrific conditions of American slavery and doubted whether many would actually affirm the equality of white and black people.[4] The fact is that in America there has always been a debate over who belongs to the civic or ecclesial community, based on race, class, gender and sexual orientation. In our time the debate over community now includes the matter of whether the created order is a part of our community in the face of an ecological crisis. Since grace is repeatedly compromised, we need to ask: What changes are needed in the principle of authority?

Sola Scriptura

In the sixteenth century, the Protestants introduced reforms regarding theology, worship, sacraments and church order. Against the authority of bishops, tradition and certain councils, they seized upon Scripture as the simplest and surest defense. If the debate was over salvation, they could appeal to the words of Jesus, Peter and Paul. If they rejected five sacraments, it was because these practices had no scriptural warrant from Jesus. In that context, appeals to the primacy of Scripture were broad and straightforward. But things quickly proved more complicated.

4. Schaff, *America*, 6–7,41–44,178, 217.

First, it soon became painfully evident that Scripture by itself could not resolve differences between Protestants. Issues regarding baptism, the Lord's Supper, the relation to the state and internal church governance became sources of division.

Second, then and now, we have been forced to admit that Scripture is not always self-evident. This constitutes a serious issue, since Protestants have relied on the assumption that certain Scriptural "truths" are clearly given. In the American tradition, this often took on a democratic formulation, assuring the free individual the right to interpret Scripture, unencumbered by class, education, wealth or priestly authority. What has emerged in our time is a greater recognition that Scripture requires a means of interpretation. Some would concede this by admitting that Luther and Calvin did not stand alone, but interpreted Scripture with Creeds and certain theological traditions. Consider for example Luther's reliance on Augustine. Others indirectly admit this by recognizing that the act of interpretation does in fact make assumptions regarding language and traditions in order to open the meaning of a given text. This produces a somewhat ironic situation. Whereas Roman Catholics have long argued that the Bible requires a community of interpretation, based on creeds and tradition, we now have Protestants converging on a similar view. To be sure, it does not affirm the absolute authority of the bishops to interpret Scripture based on specific traditions, but it does require some rephrasing in the way we speak of Scripture.

Third, in the last two centuries, major protests in the name of freedom for specific people have been compelled to go outside Scripture for authority because Scripture was either divided on the subject or controlled by those protecting the status quo. In America the obvious examples are those of black Americans and women. This produced in our time the bold declaration of a principle of authority based on the rights of dispossessed people. For some, the experience of blacks and women took precedence over certain parts of Scripture. As one might expect, this was not always received kindly by some Protestants. After centuries claiming that right doctrine had to be based on Scripture, here was an unapologetic claim that one must go outside Scripture to find the truth. To be sure, many connected the rights of blacks and women to known values within the Christian community and the Bible itself. But before we go in that direction, we need to hear the full force of this development: It is possible for Scripture to be silent on a major subject, be conflicted or be controlled by the status quo.

In fairness it also needs to be said that most Protestants have done exactly what blacks and women have done, but have not always bothered to mention it. For example, we have set aside the biblical cosmology because it did not agree with our world view. In America we have set aside preferences for monarchy in the interest of our preferences for individual freedom and democratic government. We have quietly set aside the admonition against divorce, usually hoping that no one will ask how we did that. To be sure, over time we embrace changes by connecting them to broad values like love, or liberty or equality. But note that in doing this we acknowledge that we are giving priority to the inclusion of all people even if it goes against tradition or Scripture. But what does this say about our declaration of sola scriptura?

Fourth, in the face of a modern age which challenged many aspects of traditional faith (such as the biblical cosmology, the authorship of books of the Bible as well as the historicity of certain accounts) many Protestants have sought to save the faith by protecting the authority of Scripture through the claim of biblical inerrancy. Given the priority given to Scripture among all Protestants, this may be a natural tendency (the default position), especially if Protestants had given up on rational proofs for the existence of God or the absolute authority of tradition and bishops. Such a development met the need for an absolute authority, which we might note runs parallel to the Roman Catholic appeal to an absolute authority of the pope in the rulings on faith and morals. It should also be said that for some, the appeal to an absolute Scripture was a way to avoid endless doctrinal disputes and/or subjective preferences, though it did not always settle things. The problem, however, is that what was intended as a positive solution has not resulted in greater unity but more diversity over questions as to the meaning of parts of Scripture. Nor has this approach to the Bible freed itself from endless quarrels and debates over historical/critical issues. The result is not an open and free reading of the Bible but one guided by prescribed standards which prove divisive.

Fifth, the culture wars exposed the lack of clarity regarding the meaning of *sola scriptura* among centric Protestants. Either its meaning had not been communicated to pastors and laity, or a kind of *de facto* literalism is the fallback position in times of uncertainty. In either case, centric Protestants were not ready for the Bible battles that have been waged for six decades. Pastors soon discovered that the middle of a battle over race, women, abortion or LGBTQ rights was not a good time to have a general discussion over how to interpret the Bible, especially when both sides charged the other with a selective reading of Scriptures.

All of which is to say that agreement is needed at several levels: First, we need to come together on how Scripture is authoritative while avoiding the tyranny of inerrancy and the notion that every verse is of equal value. Second, a graceful interpretation of Scripture must be owned by pastors and congregations, so that members and pastors are ready for dealing with serious issues as well as the disruptive tactics which only arouse passions. Third, special attention needs to be given to how our view of the authority of Scripture will be expressed in liturgical forms and the reading of Scripture. Announcing that the morning lesson is from "Paul's letter to the Hebrews" is not helpful. To be sure, the authorship of Hebrews is not a matter of salvation. But some level of respect and ownership needs to be given to what we actually know about Scripture.

Re-Formulating the Principle of Authority

A revised principle of authority must meet three requirements:

1. It must reflect the faith and practice of our time, including the way we actually do theology.

2. It must affirm what is the primary authority, while also giving direction to how it shall be interpreted.

3. As a general theory of authority, the proposal must clarify how other centers of authority relate to what is primary.

The Revised Proposal:

1. The primary principle is Jesus Christ, interpreted by means of grace and community.

2. This primary principle is further understood in light of multiple centers of authority, the chief being Scripture, followed by communal practice, church leaders, creeds and confessions, landmark decisions, culture, and experience.

Commentary

1. Jesus Christ as the Primary Authority

The word tradition comes from a Latin word which literally means to hand down or give over. The debate regarding faith is always over what shall be handed down, i.e., what is necessary or helpful for the life of the community. Conservatives claim that faith may only be handed down in the old forms: in the case of Roman Catholics this means the absolute truth of traditional doctrine sanctioned by an infallible pope; in the case of conservative Protestants it means holding on to the Bible as an inerrant book. Centric Protestants claim that Jesus Christ, the Word of promise, is what has been handed down to us, even as our proclamation of it has passed through several centuries of critical reflection (i.e., historical and linguistic study, changes in our view of the world and social relations). Paul's image of a treasure in earthen vessels is most appropriate: the earthen vessels may indeed change, but the treasure does not. Jesus Christ is still Lord, though the way we understand and interpret him changes. By contrast, to suggest the earthen vessels can never change is to confuse the earthen vessels with the treasure. The Bible and church doctrine may never take the place of the revelation of God in Israel and Jesus Christ, though they may indeed be faithful witnesses to it.

The best way to understand how centric Protestants came to this position is by their history. They did not wake up one day and decide to rebel against Bible and tradition. Rather, they too were nurtured on the faith of the sixteenth century reformers but in time found themselves in a world where it was not possible to base faith on claims to the inerrancy of Bible, absolute doctrine or proofs for the existence of God. Consider the following.

One has to keep in mind that the Protestant emphasis on Scripture only produced more examination of it from many directions.[5] The new science challenged the cosmology of the Bible. The historical-linguistic study raised multiple issues regarding historical details and authorship of materials. Did Paul write all the letters attributed to him? Since the nineteenth century there has been an ongoing debate over the gospels: Who wrote them? Are they biographies or confessions? Was Jesus an apocalyptic figure who was killed in conflict with the authorities? Are the sayings of Jesus

---

5. One of the ironies of John Calvin's attempt to support the authority of Scripture by pointing to the miracles and prophecies was that such an appeal encouraged rigorous historical study which was not always supportive. Cf. Calvin, *Institutes* I, VIII, 81–92.

from Jesus or do they reflect the church's remembrance of him? Throughout all of this was the serious question: To what extent can the Bible be the
basis for faith?

While Protestants accepted the Nicene and Chalcedonian affirmations
as essential for faith, the modern age raised serious concerns. In the context
of the opposing views in the fourth and fifth centuries, these creeds proved
to be faithful in affirming the NT view that God was in Christ, or that the
Word of the true God was incarnate in Jesus of Nazareth. But one concern
was that the creeds are much clearer regarding what was not acceptable
than what was actually affirmed. The continuing debates over the technical
terms *persona* and *natura* in the trinitarian debates and two *naturae* and one
persona in the christological debates illustrate the point. In many respects
modern writers found it preferable to use the biblical language of Word and
Spirit to speak of Jesus' divinity rather than the ancient category *natura*.

Added to these issues were challenges to the proofs for the existence
of God by rational argument. It no longer seemed possible to assume that
philosophical arguments would rescue faith from the debates over historical study of the Bible.

The issue for Christians in the modern age, therefore, was what stands
as the ultimate authority for faith. Those Protestants who concluded there
was no future in denying the new science or opposing historical-linguistic
study of the Bible chose an alternative consistent with the Bible, creeds and
Reformation: faith rested on the confession of Jesus Christ, the Word of
promise. Instead of taking up an endlessly defensive position that the basis
of faith is the Bible, in spite of all the difficulties it presents, they preferred
to look to Christ and his saving power. The basis for faith is Jesus Christ
and the new life he shares with believers. This did not mean a rejection of
Scripture but an affirmation of Scripture as the primary witness to Jesus
Christ. From a theological perspective, this relation of Scripture to Christ
was judged to be the way it should have been all along. One thinks of
Grünewald's painting of the crucifixion on the altar of the Isenheim chapel.[6] Christ crucified is in the center and off to the right is John the Baptist,
pointing to Jesus. Scripture points to the Word of promise, Jesus Christ.

From an historical point of view, the emphasis on a Christological
center is not surprising given the dependency of twentieth century theology on the Reformation. Luther's emphasis on the authority of Scripture
has already been discussed. Scripture is authoritative because it contains

6. Cf. Pierre Schmitt, *Isenheim Altar*, Plate 1.

the Word of promise. His *Catechism* is organized around the Ten Commandments, the Apostles Creed, the Lord's Prayer, baptism and the Lord's Supper.[7] God commands that we read the *Catechism* but the devil opposed it because there is the Word.[8] Each part of the Catechism confronts us with the Word of promise, received by faith, allowing us to trust in God alone and receive God's blessings. So he can say: "Anyone who knows the Ten Commandments perfectly knows the entire Scriptures."[9] This makes sense only because if one honors the one and true God, then one has placed all of one's trust and hope in the God who shall provide all that we need. The commandment is all about the Word of promise and faith as trust in God. In this way, the real subject of the *Catechism* and even Scripture itself is always the Word of God. John Calvin displays a similar regard for the superiority and sufficiency of Scripture in regard to idolaters, human pride and the claims of the church.[10] Scripture is authenticated by God and not the church; it is confirmed only the Spirit working in us. It is God's own witness to the truth. And, in the most memorable image, it is the spectacles given to us by God, to see truth regarding creation and salvation.[11]

These references to Scripture from Luther and Calvin must be understood in relation to two things: one is that their emphasis on Scripture must be seen in the context of the bitter struggle with church authorities which claimed the authority of tradition and bishops over against Scripture. In such a debate, one did not have to be concerned about priorities within Scripture. The second is that both Luther and Calvin lived just as the new science was emerging and before the major battles over the Bible produced by historical-linguistic studies. Given this, all sides today must project how they would have reacted in different settings. One thing is clear: both Luther and Calvin gave priority to the Word of God, or Word of promise which was found in Scripture but could not be equated with it. Given what Luther says in the *Catechism,* it is hard to imagine him saying that readers should attend to every verse of Scripture or claim that Scripture was inerrant. I would argue the same for Calvin. Consider the nature of the piety presupposed by the first question in the Heidelberg Catechism, so central to the Reformed tradition:

7. Cf. Luther, *Larger Catechism.*
8. Luther, *Catechism,* 2–9.
9. Luther, *Catechism,* 5.
10. Calvin, *Institutes* I, IV–VII, 47–81.
11. Calvin, *Institutes* I, VI, 70.

Question #1. What is your only comfort in life and in death?
Answer: That I belong, both body and soul and in life and in death,
not to myself, but to my faithful savior Jesus Christ, who has totally paid for all my sins with his precious blood, and completely
liberated me from the power of the devil, and who takes care of
me so well that not a hair can fall from my head without the will
of my Father in heaven. In fact, everything must work together for
my salvation. Besides this, by his Holy Spirit he also assures me of
eternal life and makes me wholeheartedly willing and ready to live
for him from now on.[12]

It is this christological focus which centric Protestants claim as their
primary authority. Since it reflects the nature of faith, so the form of theology corresponds to the form of faith. If faith is a matter of trust of the
heart in the grace of God revealed in Israel and Jesus Christ, then theology becomes reflection and confession of that faith. Such faith is based on
the reality of new life God has created in Jesus Christ, as manifest in the
community of believers and the world today through the Spirit. For good
reason this approach is called confessional: it relies on the power of the
Word in Jesus Christ to generate faith by the Spirit. At the same time it does
in fact rely on witnesses to faith, the primary one being Scripture itself. If
there was not a satisfactory level of credibility to Scripture in the face of
centuries of historical-linguistic study, then it would be difficult to claim
Scripture as a witness. But Scripture has retained its role as a witness and
continues to form and reform the life of Christians.

I have repeatedly made the point that centric Protestants have been
formed by three reformations: the sixteenth century, the modern age, and
the theological-biblical reforms in the twentieth century. A special word
is needed here regarding the second. It has been in the modern age that
Protestants faced a crisis. It was and is a crisis of faith, but not like that
of sin and grace. The Copernican revolution confronted believers with a
new way of viewing the world. In tandem with historical-critical studies of
the Bible and doctrinal traditions, the familiar support systems for religion
were challenged. It is hard for us to imagine the disorientation caused by
the introduction of the Copernican revolution. The changes to the ancient
cosmology assumed by the Bible appeared to shatter the harmony of the
existing order. Thinking of the sun as the center of our universe rather than
revolving around the earth requires a change in outlook.[13] Some of the

12. *Heidelberg Catechism*, 29.
13. The fact that we still speak of the sun rising and setting is interesting. Is it a

ways we thought of God, Christ, and salvation were questioned and even destroyed. What developed too often was unsettling and divisive. But faith has survived because the tradition was willing to engage in rigorous reflection and accept new ideas, primarily because it chose not to tie faith to the older systems but to direct faith to Jesus Christ, the Word of promise. Looking back at the road travelled, it is not unusual that trust in God requires changing the way we think of existing structures, be it Scripture, doctrine or ecclesial authority. Looking forward it is fair to say that we will continue to find faith and practice challenged by new ideas and voices. Our resistance to change suggests that a new crisis is not necessary but most likely inevitable. For this reason what we discovered in the past must be applied to the future: the norm is Jesus Christ rather than the ways we formulate confessions of faith and standards for practice.

What sets centric Protestants apart is the insistence on directing faith toward God in Jesus Christ, rather than the relative norms of the Bible, doctrine, or ecclesial authority. These secondary authorities cannot bear such responsibility since each reveals the limits of time and place. To claim inerrancy for the Bible is to commit the church to endless disputes and divisions over matters which are not the central point. By claiming too much for the Bible, we inevitably undermine its primary purpose, namely, to witness to the Word of God in Israel and Jesus Christ. But underlying the debate over whether Bible, creeds, tradition and church may claim absolute authority is the question whether trust should be directed toward these authorities or God alone.

This raises the question: Is the crisis of faith caused by the modern age something which all must experience? Here it is best to emphasize the positive: children and adults should be supported in looking to Jesus Christ as Lord, understood by means of grace and community. In that process there will naturally arise occasions to discuss how faith is challenged by new knowledge or the anxiety caused when faith is placed in the wrong thing. If we keep the centrality of Christ before us, rather than traditions and practices, we may be more able to deal with crises when they occur. Not everyone needs to know about the multiple authorship of the Pentateuch, or have read philosophers or key figures in the modern interpretation of the Bible. There is no need in some sophomoric way to deliberately

residual act of resistance in the face of a new cosmology or a comfortable way of combining old and new? In this regard Haydn's great work *The Creation* may illustrate how faith in a new world might still rely on biblical imagery.

pick fights with grandparents or people dying in the hospital over critical theories of the Bible.

There is, however, a need for children and adults bearing responsibility in family, church and the world, to be aware of how we interpret the Bible in light of Jesus Christ, rather than in a literal or legalistic way. Given the world we live in, it is hard to imagine that one might grow to maturity in faith without some form of crisis caused by doubt or challenge to things which have supported us, be it the Bible, creed or persons around us.

But we should be quick to add that the solution is not a prescribed three step process which can be controlled by teachers, preachers or the community. Indeed, it is also the case that Jesus disrupts our lives and the way we would order the world. He makes it very clear that we may not come into the kingdom as we are, or attempt to order the kingdom according to our standards. In this way the crisis of faith has often occurred when we had to deal with issues of justice and peace.

Here let me give an example of staying with the power of the gospel rather than being distracted by the temptation to defend traditional authorities. What may surprise some is that the example involves meeting Billy Graham. In terms of official affiliation, Graham was clearly the representative of conservative Protestants who insisted on the fundamentals of faith and an inerrant Bible. At one point he ran a column in daily newspapers where people would send in questions about the Bible and, no matter how difficult, an answer would be given to explain why the passage did not involve any contradictions or difficulties. That was the traditionalist side of Graham's organization, always wanting to differentiate itself from so called liberal Protestants by insisting that faith requires an inerrant Bible. But in his preaching Graham struck a quite different tone. He seldom spent time arguing about the Bible or defending conservative interpretations. Instead he had the courage to ask people whether they believed in God, or, in his signature style, to ask them whether they ". . . have a personal relation with Jesus Christ."

I always wondered how this more evangelical side of Graham related to the conservative, so insistent on opposing the modern world. Graham answered the question when he spoke at Harvard Divinity School when I was there in the 1960s. The announcement of the event prompted both liberal and conservative students to wonder what he would say in this bastion of liberal studies. To a full house Graham went to the podium and spent thirty minutes talking about grace. Now one must consider the context: graduate programs are demanding and competitive, with little support for students trying to find their way. One worked six to seven days a week all year long. In spirit and substance the atmosphere was more about law than gospel. In that situation, Graham disarmed those looking for a fight by speaking a word of grace to those in need. The point is that here we see the distinction between trying to transmit the tradition by defensiveness regarding what is handed down in contrast to confessing the good news of the gospel. Everyone expected Graham to get tied up in knots over details relating to the historical-critical interpretation of the Bible, when in fact he went straight to the issue of our need. Was he advised by insiders to take this approach simply for strategic reasons? Did I wish Graham would object to the legalism of fundamentalism and the endless quarrels over details regarding the Bible? Did I hope that he might throw his influence behind the cause of racial justice and women's rights rather than accepting the status quo? Of course! But on that day I did wonder whether he saw that Christianity would not be saved by defensiveness but by claiming the gospel.

2. Grace and Community

This proposal posits Jesus Christ as the primary authority, in contrast to one or more of the other authorities we rely upon. But Jesus Christ is affirmed by all Christians and can be interpreted in many different ways. In America the term too often refers to a religion "all about me," separated from the community of Christ. It is tied to authoritative structures which restrict the grace of Christ, depending on compliance with church rules. Compare the discussion among Roman Catholic bishops to exclude political leaders from the sacrament. For years some find reference to Jesus Christ abhorrent because it is a symbol of Christians who stand for the exclusion of minorities and women from full membership in the church. The principle of authority must include some designation what is meant by Jesus Christ.

Two words are offered to do this: first, grace as the affirmation of God's will to create and redeem the world; second, community, as the goal of God's redemptive action. These two words are chosen for their positive value and for the way they speak to the challenges of our time. As argued in earlier chapters, in our time the gospel is denied and subverted by legalism and individualism, by authoritarianism and exclusion of so many people. Grace and community point to the means and the ends of the gospel. To say this does not mean that Scripture is being rejected. It continues as the fundamental witness to Jesus Christ. But everyone claims Scripture and, unfortunately, it has been used as an instrument of oppression. While Scripture was the obvious standard to differentiate Protestants from Roman Catholics, the current debate with conservative Protestants is over the meaning of Scripture. Toward this end, the proposal places Jesus Christ at the center and secondarily affirms grace and community.

3. Multiple Centers of Authority

This proposal affirms that in addition to a primary authority, we must give attention to the way other authorities function in the life of faith and practice. In one sense this may appear as counter-productive: having set forth the fundamental standard, one now proposes that there are others which qualify it or assist in interpreting it. The reasons for this are quite simple: this is in fact how we live and think in faith and practice; instead of pretending that this is not the case, it is helpful to affirm it and explore how these centers of authority function for us. Consider the following:

a. Communal practice. Certain things in the life of the church (e.g., worship, leadership, the sacraments, and moral practice) have authority by their connection with Jesus, the apostles or long standing practice.

b. Church leaders. The NT refers to several kinds of leaders: those with oversight (*episcope*), presbyters, and deacons, indicating that quite early there was a need for leaders to guide the community. The importance of a connection to Jesus is seen in the authority given to the Apostles, namely, those called and sent by Jesus. How and why leaders would be invested with authority was a crucial issue for the Reformation, as illustrated by the multiple forms of church governance which emerged. We do well to include teachers as leaders, since history reveals a longstanding tension between bishops and teachers of the church, as Luther discovered.

c. Written documents. With the development of a Christian canon of writings, parallel to Hebrew scriptures, the churches recognized the authority of writings connected to the apostles bearing witness to Jesus Christ.

d. Creeds and confessions summarize the faith and in some cases settle disputes. Most Protestants continued the tradition of writing short or long confessions.

e. Landmark decisions. Some of the great debates in the church were settled by decisions by an individual or council. We see this in Scripture itself, as in decisions by Paul, or in creeds like the Nicene Creed. Landmark decisions attempt to give direction and many have survived for centuries because they are judged to be faithful witnesses to Jesus Christ.

f. Culture, which provides the physical and social environment in which the church lives. Every culture presents churches with issues regarding social, economic and political traditions, as well expecting citizens to be loyal, participate in military service and pay taxes.

g. Experience. Individuals and groups have always drawn upon their experience to interpret faith and practice. In the community of Christ neither the individual nor the majority have absolute rights, but the community must be open to the affirmations growing out of experience.

The mere fact that a discussion of the primary authority would also recognize other authorities is liberating and upsetting. How shall all these authorities be related to one another and to the primary authority? The answer is that there is no simple set of rules or procedures. The fact is that specific issues generate different appeals for support. Evidence for the heliocentric view of the universe was based on scientific arguments and Christians had to decide whether to accept or deny it. Perhaps the experience of explorers circumnavigating the world impressed people. Some decisions, such as those regarding Marcion, Arius and Pelagius, were based on appeals to Scripture and Christian experience. In the case of liberty and equality regarding black people and women, or the ordination of women, you find appeals to tradition, the Bible, moral and cultural values as well as experience. These debates also revealed that Scripture can be used by both sides, again pressing the issue whether there is a primary value in Scripture. While introducing multiple centers of authority may seem to complicate things, in fact it is a step forward to recognize them because that is how we actually make decisions.

For this theory to work, it must deal with three challenges: The first is to find ways to incorporate a christological view of authority into minds and hearts of members and congregations. The last fifty years have revealed, not surprisingly, that a significant part of centric Protestants either lean toward, or embrace a literal view of Scripture. This has complicated discussions regarding faith and practice, simply because in the heat of battle there is no interest to have a general discussion of Scripture. If leadership has not helped members navigate the troubled waters of Bible interpretation before debates over civil rights, abortion, gay rights or women's rights, the debates become even more acrimonious and divisive. In part the problem is that some form of inerrancy is probably the natural tendency of churches which have placed so much emphasis on Scripture. For centuries they have used it as a defense against Roman Catholic criticism, so why doesn't it work as the authority for everything? More time and attention must be given to the way we present Scripture readings and use it in worship, education and study. For example, when we refer to Scripture as "the Word of the Lord," what message is being conveyed to the congregation? The more we are silent on how books of the Bible came to be and how we interpret them, the more we will generate clergy and laity who do not share a christological norm in reading the Bible. We need to review, therefore, how we testify to what is authoritative in all aspects of the church's life with people of every age.

A second challenge is to examine church governance in light of what we take to be authoritative. This is complicated by the way values become set against one another. One the one hand, American culture values liberty and democratic process, but on the other we are reminded that the kingdom of God is not a democracy. This tension produces considerable turmoil in the life of churches. Consider again that the individualism of our culture elevates the individual over traditional authorities. In the eighteenth century such authorities were symbolized by monarchs, bishops, and tradition. Running through the last sixty years has been a rebellion against all established authorities, be it government, national religious institutions, corporations, public schools, university establishments and even medical experts. This appeared to erupt with a vengeance in the election of 2016. If traditional politics was a debate between liberal and conservative approaches to government, the new divide appears to present a debate between all established authority and those seeking elected office in order to destroy established authority. This raises multiple issues for church governance. Can a church operate with a top-down structure, relying upon traditional authority or even claims to special knowledge? What impact will the American suspicion of authority have upon churches, which inevitably make claims to what is authoritative? Looking forward, can the attempt to renew centric Protestant churches succeed without developing more inclusive and non-hierarchal systems of governance? But even this is not an easy task, since majority rule can be as divisive as appeals to tradition and bishops. For decades we have sought to employ a political model of rules of order to resolve contested issues, with the result that groups are divided by 55–60 percent versus 40–45 percent. Is that helpful for the long run? How shall strategies for rebuilding the church deal with memberships too often divided over what both sides consider to be essentials?

A third challenge is to demonstrate how the proposed theory of authority allows us to confess Jesus Christ and made decisions in the life of the church. To begin with, this means that the confession of Jesus Christ should not only define the basis of our unity but also nurture it. It would also mean that the ability to deal with difficult issues will in a large measure depend on the trust and commitment among members themselves and members and the ordained leaders before the debates start.

5

Worship and the Vital Center

RENEWAL FOR CENTRIC PROTESTANTS must begin by reclaiming the vital center of the tradition. This requires choices, since members diverge by assuming Christ's real presence in the multiple forms which differentiate Christians: e.g., Word and faith, sacraments, spiritual rebirth, the reconciled community, works of love and justice and solidarity with Christ who is with those who suffer. All of these responses are found in Christian communities as a distinctive form of the church. From a strategic perspective, however, it is imperative for centric Protestants to begin with communal worship where the presence of Christ is affirmed in Word and sacrament. The challenge we face is whether there will be communities formed by grace and united by Christ in this world as a witness to the gospel. In this tradition, worship as proclamation of the Word and celebration of our union with Christ is the primary act which sustains and inspires witness and service.

This proposal rests on the general argument presented thus far: Centric Protestants constitute a distinct and necessary voice among Christians in North America. They comprise a cluster of denominations rooted in the sixteenth century Reformation, further shaped by the critical thinking of the modern age regarding the world and Christian traditions. They have been further reformed by the theological revolutions and challenges of the twentieth century. The starting point has always been grace and in the last century grace has been coupled with community. Since grace and community are derived and given substance by God's action in Jesus Christ, it has been further argued that the principle of authority must be defined from a christological perspective.

The attempt to describe centric Protestants has had to take into account sixty years of decline and loss. Without rehearsing all that was said, several issues are pertinent to what we shall present here.

- Centric Protestants discovered that American culture was not as hospitable to Christian faith as some assumed: the culture is dominated by individualism and materialism; it has sanctioned forms of inequality detrimental to Christian community. It has also encouraged the assault on nature to the point where we now face an ecological crisis.

- Centric Protestants find themselves surrounded by conservative religious traditions marked by authoritarianism and legalism, all the while opposing much of the modern world.

- Centric Protestants did not help matters by inactivity regarding evangelism or relying on a message of unconditional love without a call to discipleship. In worship they retained the medieval framework focusing on sin and forgiveness, being quite slow to complete the reform of the Lord's Supper begun in the sixteenth century.

Taken together we have a tradition in need of returning to its only treasure while struggling with internal problems which detract from it. This then becomes the challenge: if the tradition is to be revived, it must recover its vital center, not in a safe place shielded from the crisis but in the midst of all the things which subvert its life. What is proposed here as the last challenge is simply this: to discover again the power of the gospel in communal worship.

A. Three Liturgical Traditions

Liturgies express and give structure to a specific vision of the vital center. In the medieval worship of Luther's time, this would involve affirming the real presence of Christ in the bread and wine, shared with believers for the forgiveness of sins and the celebration of union with Christ. The liturgy, therefore, must create a framework for the recitation of the history of salvation and the consecration of the bread and wine, leading up to the sharing of the body and blood of Christ. Such a liturgy provides multiple ways in which the congregation is incorporated into this story, through invitation, confession of sin, hearing Scripture and homily, the praise of God and the creed. Most important, the liturgy must be priestly, whereby the leader, ordained by a bishop by the authority of the bishop of Rome, determines who is invited and sets before us bread and wine transformed by prayer and the power of the Spirit into the body and blood of Christ. The liturgy of the Mass is not accidentally thrown together, but represents a carefully crafted movement of words, acts, bread and wine, and music—all of which bring Christ to us and us to Christ. Something is happening there at the table by the power of the Spirit, which we by grace, prayer and dedication of heart, may partake.

In its Anglican version, just about all of these aspects of the liturgy are maintained with the exception that Cranmer followed Luther's rejection of transubstantiation. Nevertheless, he created a revised service which incorporates so much of the medieval tradition as well as aspects from many reformers, that the result was a big tent which allowed just about all of the traditions to see in the new liturgy what they saw as essential.[1] This explains why, in the present situation, former Roman Catholics may participate in the Episcopal liturgy along with persons drawn from the spectrum of Protestantism and all find it acceptable. There is still the story of salvation, leading up to the transaction of our offerings to Christ, the forgiveness of sins by the sharing of the body and blood of Christ, administered by priests in robes even more splendid than their Roman brethren.

The liturgy of centric Protestants developed in a different way because the purpose of worship is defined by a theology of the Word. This may be expressed in either a liturgy of the Word or liturgy of the table, or the two together. For our purposes we shall call this a *low church* liturgy. The internal dynamic is no longer a transaction but the alternation between *proclamation* of the promise of grace and the congregation's *response* of faith and gratitude. The former will require the reading of Scripture and sermon while the latter requires prayers of praise and thanksgiving, confession of faith and a new hymnody. All this will be integrated and developed in a variety of ways if one surveys liturgies of Lutherans and Reformed, Presbyterians, United Methodists, Black Churches and Anabaptists. In some the iconoclastic impulse will be more dominant, as in the simplicity of Congregational and Mennonite buildings. There will be among most a

1. Cf. the fuller discussion of the Anglican reform in Schmiechen, *Gift and Promise: An Evangelical Theology of the Lord's Supper*, 64–69.

deliberate concern for ordained ministry, though always balanced by Luther's affirmation of the priesthood of believers and the tendency to think of ordination in functional terms rather than as a higher state of being.

A third form in America is somewhat hard to name, since it takes different forms in various times. In one instance there is revivalism, which develops what I would call an open liturgy aimed at drawing people into the hearing of the good news and believing. In the last half century the open liturgy found expression in mega churches and TV preaching, which often downplay any connection with traditional symbols, the institutional church or sacraments. The purpose of the liturgy—deliberately undefined in any formal way—is to welcome people into a time of hearing the good news by word and song without raising anxieties regarding their lack of knowledge or prior membership. Instead the key is to present a message of Christ to transform and enrich their lives. If the Roman Mass makes clear that the action is at the altar/table where Christ is present whether anyone beside the priest is there or listening, in this liturgy the action is from the speaker to the listener. In one sense it all depends on how the preacher delivers the message and the believer's response.

Each of these liturgical traditions has certain values as well as ties to religious and social history, which can work for or against it. In the case of the high church tradition, the first thing to be mentioned is the sense of spiritual presence conveyed by the liturgy and the way the sanctuary is laid out. One becomes aware of the fact that it does not all depend on the priest or persons in attendance to convey a sense of the holy. We are invited into an experience of wonder, mystery and the sacred. Second, these liturgies give structure to the remembrance of salvation history. This is re-enforced by the stability of certain parts of the liturgy, which over time are committed to memory. Scripture, prayers and doxologies become internal to the soul. Third, high church liturgies present the gospel in a variety of ways, appealing to all of our senses as well as heart and head. It may surprise many Protestants that many Episcopal churches read all four lessons in the lectionary. Reading the gospel from the center aisle adds a graceful note: even before the sermon begins the Word is in the midst of the people of God. Sermon, liturgy, music and Eucharist present the gospel in multiple ways. At the same time, Roman Catholics still struggle with the purpose of the homily. In September, 2021 Pope Francis urged priests to keep it under ten minutes. It is clearly not the indispensable proclamation of the gospel, the center piece of worship, but a brief meditation on the lectionary with practical advice. Roman Catholics and Episcopalians also bear the weight of state church traditions, which required major adjustments in America. They are also highly traditional and authoritarian, which has created major problems for Roman Catholics regarding the role of women in church and in the current crisis over sexual abuse of children by priests. One irony is that the very traditionalism of Episcopalians has now placed them in a position of offering a counter-cultural liturgy steeped in wonder, mystery and tradition in the face of a secularized and pragmatic world.

The open liturgical tradition has also encountered twists and turns. After a long history of being subordinate to other more established traditions (except in the South), the open tradition now emerges as the dominant Protestant position, prompting it to depart from its long standing principle of separation of church and state. As a liturgical form, it has had a major impact on Protestantism in several ways: First, it has been very successful in welcoming people—church and non-church—to its services. Whether this has to do with the lack of Christian symbols, or the absence of creedal and doctrinal formulations, is not clear. But somehow people are welcomed and anticipate something. Second, the use of TV has expanded its influence far beyond denominational membership. Third, parallel to the creation of revivals, the seeker services and so-called contemporary worship services constitute two of the most successful innovations in recent decades. Finally, by presenting a speaker, without liturgical robes, standing alone on a stage holding a Bible and microphone, this tradition claims authority directly from God through the Bible. Tradition, church authority, ordination and education are all secondary to personal authority directly derived from God. Using the terms of Jack Carroll's analysis of religious authority, one would call this *personal authority* in contrast to *official authority*. Note he further divides such authority between *representing the sacred* and *expertise*.[2] But these gains have too often been tied to fundamentalism and anti-intellectualism, marked by authoritarianism and legalism. As a result there are many alienated from religion because of the harm done. As religious refugees, they are not sure these new measures are gains for the gospel. Somewhat different is the religion on TV (e.g., Peale, Schuler and Osteen) which has contributed to what I would call American popular religion which is "all about me." It has played down the gospel of the cross and played up a religion of personal happiness and wealth. Centric Protestants

2. Carroll, *One With Authority*, 57. We might do well to ask how leaders in low-church services display personal authority, especially in terms of representing the sacred.

tend to dismiss conservative TV religion but it should be remembered that it is basically the only Protestant religion on TV and viewed by many before attending centric Protestant churches. We should also note that in the popular mind, TV has given Americans only three images of worship: services from the National Cathedral in Washington (Episcopal), revivals/ megachurches, and funerals at black churches.

The great strength of centric Protestants is their insistence that worship be tied to proclamation of the Word calling forth a response in faith and love. But alongside this priority of the Word is an embrace of the world. This has played out in openness to the Enlightenment and the development of democratic institutions in America. The sacred dance of religion, therefore, not only involved the polarity of sin and grace, but also of reason and religion, as well as prayer and social activism. It is not an accident that people struggling with the challenges of the Enlightenment, with new political forms, with expansion of the nation and great social struggles, were inspired by a form of worship that alternated between hearing the Word and finding new ways to embody the community of Christ in the world. By mid-twentieth century they represented a Protestant religious establishment, with churches on *Main St.* closely tied to social, political, educational and economic institutions. This involved ties to the elitism of the educated classes, a bias toward ideas over experience, and involvement in controversial social change.

How things went into decline still generates differences of opinion. Perhaps the decline was already prefigured in the popular consensus that religious America consisted of Protestant, Catholic and Jew, which is to say that America was no longer a mainline Protestant nation. Was it complacency and/or reliance on ethnic ties which no longer bound people to historic churches—be they English, Scots, Scandinavian or German? Was it the inability to respond with programs of persuasion directed at our children or evangelism directed toward the unchurched? Some thought the problem was spirituality, though the tradition was slow to ask why and how so many could be religious outside the church. For example, in the face of the decline of college graduates attending seminaries, many treated this as a labor force issue (i.e., supply and demand of leaders) rather than a faith crisis. Since some perceived no need for more clergy, the issue was ignored. But should we have asked why so few young people were responding to a vision of leadership in churches? The tradition was also tied to the activism which generated the long culture war and controversial social changes. But even here there is no agreement on how this affected the decline. Was the decline a result of turning attention and funds to witness outside the church or just not attending to the care of congregations? Conservative traditions were quite willing to name reasons for the decline. Roman Catholic critics saw the decline stemming from the freedom to believe as one wants and the rejection of the Roman Mass. Conservative Protestants see the decline as a result of the failure to adhere to their fundamentals and conservative policies. It is ironic that the criticisms sent mixed signals: on the one hand, pastors were encouraged to become more spiritual and recover a sense of wonder and sense of the sacred; on the other hand they were told to adopt a more free and open style of worship using contemporary music and seeker services, with less reliance on arcane symbols and doctrines of the institutional church. But if one cannot be certain why the loss of leadership in American religion occurred, how can one be sure of the way to recovery?

Locating centric Protestants in the American religious scene is relevant since recovery must take place in the midst of this alignment. The divergence between these traditions becomes evident when we ask the simple question regarding worship: What is happening? In high church forms, at the center is a transaction on which our salvation depends. For the open church, at the center is the decision believers make which determines their future in heaven or hell. For centric Protestants, the center involves the dynamics of Word and faith. To speak of the Word is to speak of the presence of Christ, offering the promise of life. This life is generated and nurtured by grace and community, in the context of the kingdom of God confronting the kingdoms of this world. What is at stake is not simply my salvation, but the redemption of the whole world and the reconciliation of all peoples. It makes a difference whether people show up, because the promise of grace anticipates the response of faith, love and hope. Something is indeed happening: The Word stands in opposition to the idols of this world and we are called to participate in the new life. Here there is a message of life in the face of death, but it is always tied to the transformation of our lives and the world by the cross and resurrection, a new covenant and the coming of the kingdom.

When the vital center is described in this way, we may risk formulating the problem: If this is what is happening in worship, why haven't people come? For the sake of discussion, there are many possibilities: At one end of the spectrum there are questions as to whether the message has been unclear or confused. The most basic question is whether we have consistently and effectively sought to have worship witness to the vital center named as the celebration of Word and faith. Then come concerns that members are so much a part of the modern world that the action is elsewhere. While this might take the form of defining the purpose of life in worldly pursuits, it can also take religious form by seeing one's vocation in noble endeavors apart from the church. Still other concerns suggest that religious language has lost is power, or that too many people have reverted to deism, where God may exist but is not present and we may not expect anything. In the worst case, there is the possibility that many don't believe in God anymore, or at least the God described in traditional Christianity. While these possibilities move in different directions, they point to one need, namely, the tradition needs to be clear about the message and present it with persuasion. But let us remember: God is not a marketing strategy. God does not exist because we want people to attend worship. At the same time, if we believe the message, then it falls upon us to proclaim in word and deed that God is in our midst as the God who raised the crucified to be Lord and has created on earth a redeemed community for the sake of all people. The message is not a postcard from heaven: "Wish you were here. Love, God." People can receive that message in their homes, or work or favorite outdoor spot. The same can be said for the popular message of unconditional love. There must be a compelling reason for people to attend, listen, share, be joyful, commit to serve and take comfort in a blessing. We again come back to the question: What's happening? Roman Catholics tell us that Christ is in the bread and wine on the altar; conservative Protestants tell us you need to be there for your eternal salvation. What do we say is happening?

B. Centric Protestants and the Vital Center

If our worship is inspired by Jesus Christ, the vital center, then it must involve: (1) an encounter with the Word of promise; (2) an invitation to participate in the story of sin and salvation; (3) the celebration of gratitude and joy.

1. The Encounter with the Word of Promise

The reformers were clear: worship is an encounter with the Word, understood as the promise of grace received by trust of the heart. Something is indeed happening: we are invited into the presence of God to be called, addressed, and challenged for the sake of celebrating the new life Christ brings in the community of grace on earth. It is the encounter with God where we are claimed as the people of God and called to be witnesses on earth. Now of course, this encounter is expressed in different ways as the presence of God, or the naming of God as Father, Son and Holy Spirit, or as Christ the living Word, or as the life-giving Spirit which binds us together. In each case, what is happening is not confined to the words and actions of the pastor/preacher or the lector or the musicians and choir. What is happening is coming into the presence of God. If this is the case, then each part of the service must be reviewed from this perspective.

The first question must be: Does the opening of the service affirm that we are in the presence of Christ? It is striking that in the Lord's Supper, the liturgy specifically begins with the recognition that it is Christ who invites us to the table. It is his table, we are his guests and he gives us his gifts. The movement is from God in Christ to us, not from us to Christ. But in the service of the Word things are not so clear. In actual practice, there is considerable variation in how the service of the Word shall begin. This leads to mixed signals whether we are being summoned by God or the pastor or the choir. For example, services may begin with a trinitarian declaration, words of adoration and praise, a prayer of invocation, i.e., calling upon God to be present, or words to gather people together in the name of Christ. But which is it? Are we summoned by God or are we hosting the service and asking God or Christ to join us? It would be consistent with our theology to begin by gathering in the presence of the One who is already and always there, in the presence of the Christ who announced the coming of the kingdom, died and rose, only to promise that he would be with us always. It makes a difference. If we are hosting the event, then it all depends on us—the liturgist's ability to fashion words which awaken us or the preacher's ability to find a topic and present it in such a way that we respond in faith, hope and love. But if we are invited into an encounter with the Word of promise, then the real issue is how do we communicate that expectation to those gathered by the design of the space, our location, music, symbolic acts and words spoken. This also requires that we are ready to respond to the Word which gives life.

Once past the opening lines, what should come next? In many churches the opening moves quickly to a hymn of praise (if it has not already occurred during a processional) followed by a confession of sin. But here again, we must ask: why? At times this is simply justified by appealing to tradition, though it is doubtful many know what that is. Or it is often justified by reference to Isaiah 6, where the majesty and holiness of God prompt the confession of unworthiness and sin. This introduces a motif which will be common to worship: coming into God's presence requires the acknowledgement of our unworthiness, followed by forgiveness and a divine call: "Whom shall I send, and who will go for us?" This in turn prompts the response: "Here am I! Send me." This is a favorite text for ordination services, though it may not be as appropriate as one thinks. In Isaiah 6:9–13 God tells Isaiah that the message is total destruction. Aside from that problem, if this is a rationale for moving quickly from the opening declaration to the confession of sin, it supports the medieval framework where sin and forgiveness dominate worship. In earlier chapters it was argued that Luther wanted to change the direction of the movement in worship, from our gifts and pleas for mercy offered up to God to God's gracious descent to us in mercy. The problem is that Protestants still kept the general framework of sin-forgiveness for the service. So, whether it is an appeal to tradition, or Isaiah 6 or a remnant from the medieval Mass, our worship services have tended to join the opening sentences with a call to confession of sin.

For us in our time, we must ask: After the opening sentence, what is the first word we wish the pastor to speak to the congregation? The issue is not whether a confession of sin should be in the service, but when. After the call to worship, what is the most needed word? Consider the following issues:

- What does it mean to gather in worship in a world operating on secular and pragmatic assumptions, where people feel divided, anxious and stressed? Do we really think people obligated by work, parenting, family issues and even world events can turn all that off by a one sentence declaration from the minister? Looking at the matter from the point of view of a faith crisis, where faith has waned or is unsure, what is the best way to engage people? These questions prompt one to wonder if the first word should be asking the congregation to confess our sins. The questions also suggest that we need a major review of the act of gathering.

- There are other forms of call and response besides Isaiah 6. For example, consider the call of Abraham, or Moses. In some cases the call to serve or be changed is preceded by a gift or event in the world. The obvious example is Jesus' declaration that the kingdom of God is at hand, leading to the call for a response. (Mark 1:14) While this verse does not tell us what the kingdom is, what follows in the gospels does.

This suggests that our ability to repent is really dependent on hearing the Word of grace in Scripture and sermon.

- Luther spoke of repentance as a life-long task. If that is the case, then it probably needs to be integrated into other aspects of the service which call for prayer, transformation and renewal. For example, for some the act of repentance may appear not in answering whether we have sinned but in volunteering to help others.

These comments suggest two challenges: First, there is a need to find ways to make clear to all that worship is an encounter with the God who has redeemed us in Christ. Most of the people being addressed have already been baptized! Does that change anything? What other acts, prayers or Scripture would assist in affirming the presence of Christ? Second, there is a need to reconsider the act of Gathering from the standpoint of contemporary believers in a world gone crazy. Now is the time to convene liturgists, pastors, preachers, theologians, musicians and lay leaders to reform the moments of Gathering from the stand point of grace and community.

2. Inviting People into the Story of Sin and Salvation

When I was a child the celebration of Lent was a very somber time. Jesus' sufferings and death were always before us. But what was especially important was the way the congregation was invited to participate in the stories of Jesus, the disciples and the people around him, including Jesus' enemies. They all were singled out and examined in terms of their motives, confusion, ambition, lack of faith and fear. One did not have to be too bright to see oneself in all the characters, be it James and John, Peter, the Samaritan woman, or even King Herod. We were also expected to see our lives in terms of Jesus' temptations, fear and fidelity. It was a theatre in the round, or perhaps a modern version of medieval stained glass windows depicting the events of Jesus' life. Jesus' story became our story and something was expected of us.

In leading worship in our time, what specifically is needed to draw people into the drama of sin and salvation?

- We need to tell the story of the cross and resurrection. Here we see the judgment of God against the sin of the world as well as God's vindication of the crucified to be Lord. In his fidelity to God and his suffering with us, Jesus reveals the God who is with us and for us.

- We need to be willing to unveil the idols of this world. In the Baptismal liturgy, parents and godparents are asked whether they renounce the evils of this world. But we never ask which ones! Evangelical worship must name those things which exclude some from our midst, those things which dehumanize or which generate violence, or which promise happiness and peace while betraying the promise. To fail to name the idols is to ignore what is happening in the lives of people and miss the opportunity of proclaiming the new life in Christ.

- We need to proclaim an eschatological vision. Here we must acknowledge that centric Protestants have been so opposed to the endless apocalyptic predictions—both ancient and modern—that they have surrendered the field to right wing speculation about the end of the world, natural disasters or terrifying political events. But we cannot live without a vision of the future. While there are instances of apocalyptic language in the gospels and the Book of Revelation, in general the NT prefers to interpret cross and resurrection in terms of the history of salvation regarding sin, death and powers of this world. The future is defined not in terms of cosmic dualism but in terms of what God has promised. We are to pray and hope for the kingdom of God and the reconciliation and unity of all things in Christ. (Ephesians 1–2)

If inviting people into the drama of sin and salvation involves these themes, what would we do differently? In general we need clarity of purpose and the union of all the elements into a cohesive form. Here let us look first at Scripture, then the sermon.

Worship defined by the Word of promise will obviously involve the reading of Scripture. But there is a wide range of practices regarding how this is done. The common lectionary has the advantage of reading from all parts of the Bible and not letting the choices rely on the pastor's favorite parts of the Bible. But there are times when the lectionary choices are unusual. In August, 2021 the gospel lessons for three Sundays were from John 6, with unusual gaps and overlap in the readings. Without opening a great debate regarding the importance of this chapter for sacramental theology, are three Sundays really needed? We also need to ask how a set schedule prepared years in advance allows us to deal with a time of crisis—either regarding the crisis of the church or the crisis of the world (e.g., Ukraine, 2022).

There is also the matter of whether congregations actually read all four assigned readings? As noted, it may be that high church Episcopalians, with weekly Eucharist, are more consistent in reading all four lessons than their Protestant neighbors. I have been in services where the readings were reduced to one, used as the text for the sermon. Such practice sends mixed messages about how and when Scripture is important. Where, how and when Scripture is read also needs attention. Episcopalians give us several practices which are striking: one is bringing a Bible into the service raised high in the procession of choir and priests; another is reading the gospel from the center aisle, affirming the Word in the midst of the congregation. A third is chanting the Psalms instead of having them read to us. Finally, if four passages are to be read, do they all have to be read at the same time or could they be read throughout the service?

Given such variety of practice, would it be helpful to consider again why and how Scripture should function in worship. It appears that the lectionary was designed for normal times to present breadth and depth in readings throughout the church year. Given the fact that these are not normal times—for the church or the world—do we need a new lectionary that would support pressing needs: texts for the drama of salvation, for affirming faith in troubled times, or for people who know little about Scripture—be they members or seekers—and alternative readings for crisis.

The sermon also presents us with challenges: Historically, Protestants seized upon the sermon as proclamation of the Word of promise, often providing lengthy sermons for edification as well as the nurture of faith. Pope Francis recently emphasized the difference between Protestant sermons and a Roman Catholic homily by encouraging priests to keep the homily to less than ten minutes—a suggestion greeted by his listeners with applause! His suggestion reflects the assumption that the sacrament is the centerpiece and that the homily is not an equal presentation of the Word. By contrast, Protestant sermons proclaim the Word of promise, and for this reason were equated with the Lord's Supper. One could have a service of the Word without a service of the table. But if this is the case, then we need to review the relation of the sermon to Scripture.

In general, Protestants have tied the sermon to Scripture in order to keep sermons close to the witness to grace. Textual preaching became normative in order to avoid topical sermons, reflecting the preacher's favorite themes. But it is fairly easy to announce a text and then use it as a springboard into favorite themes. On the other hand, can a topical sermon be scriptural by carefully tying a topic to scriptural sources? We also saw the emergence of narrative preaching, in contrast to topical and didactic sermons, in order to draw people into the narratives in the gospels. Then we discovered even such a method could end up with entertaining stories which caught our attention on Sunday morning but left us wondering the next day what was the point. Yet another problem is that preaching on the lectionary, which offers short passages from one chapter, runs the risk of focusing attention on smaller and smaller sections of the Bible. Which is to say, how do we assure that textual preaching will produce bold proclamation of the gospel for our time?

There are also problems created when sermons assume grace takes only one form, namely the forgiveness of sins. As noted earlier, many listeners are not overwhelmed by a sense of guilt caused by their actions but by shame and the limitations forced on them. If we never affirm that the gospel means liberation as well as forgiveness, a major portion of the congregation is ignored. The gospel also speaks of reconciliation of people, the recovery of the knowledge of God, freedom from the idols of this world, and the restoration of the earth. The question then is: Can we develop an evangelical form of preaching which will celebrate the many forms of grace?

This brings us to two crucial issues: the purpose and location of the sermon in the context of worship as a whole. Put in simple terms: How does the sermon relate to what is happening in worship? Thus far worship has been defined as the encounter of the Word of promise calling forth a response of faith. If that is the case, then two things follow:

First, the vital center of worship is the presence of Christ, whereby he gathers us together and shares the gifts of new life. The sermon is not the center of the service, Jesus Christ and his promise are. Once again the image of John the Baptist pointing to the crucified Christ comes to mind. But how shall such a view of preaching take liturgical form, if not by insisting that the sermon point to God's saving power in Jesus Christ as it impinges on the world and our lives. In this sense, the formal descriptions of sermons as textual, topical, or narrative must be subordinated to the material description, i.e., proclaiming Christ by means of grace and community. The test of such preaching would not be the greatest knowledge about the text and its background, but the authenticity of the words spoken—no matter how short in length—by the preacher and their ability to invite listeners into the story of Jesus.

Second, the invitation into the story of Jesus requires a response from those gathered. Worship should embody the dialectic of Word and faith, call and response. The gospel is not simply the story of Jesus but also the story about how the promise has given us new life, transforming us by turning us to God and taking on what Paul calls the mind of Christ. In other words, worship must also be about the process of changing us and allowing us to discover what that change means in relation to the story of Jesus.

Before we become embroiled in debates on how to do this on Sunday mornings, with charges of re-introducing the anxious bench from nineteenth-century revivalism, let us be reminded of Calvin's opening words from the *Institutes* that all knowledge includes the knowledge of God and the knowledge of ourselves; moreover, we may not always know which comes first.[3] Such words give us the freedom to speak of our hearts and minds as well as the story of Jesus. They also protest against any formalism which assumes that there is only one right way to speak of the good news. If the Word is to point to Christ, then it is fitting for listeners to respond to Christ as believers struggling to be faithful.

Consider a moment of illumination which occurred when reading a column by David Brooks in the *New York Times*. He noted that in our time people use personal stories to define themselves. He then asked: "Yet if the quality of our self-stories is so important, where do we go to learn the craft of self-narration? Shouldn't there be some institution that teaches us to revise our stories through life, so we don't have to suffer for years and wind up in therapy?"[4] Is not the answer to this question, for Jews and Christians, the synagogue and the church?

This is to suggest that Christian worship is the place where our self-stories are told, judged, revised and rewritten in light of the story of Jesus Christ. The classic images of repentance, being born again, dying and rising with Christ, or taking on the mind of Christ all point to the necessity of change by the power of the Spirit in hearts and minds. Put in another way, we are not talking about enhancing or completing our stories, but *deconstructing* our stories and being re-formed by the story of Jesus. For this reason, communal worship is important, since we need the support of fellow members who give us the courage to tell our stories and admit how much we are in need. The catalyst for change is the preaching of the cross and resurrection, or reference to idols of this world or God's purpose for our lives.

When we tell our stories outside the context of the dialectic of Word and faith, then we end up talking about ourselves. In such situations,

3. Calvin, *Institutes*, Bk. 1, Ch. I, 35.
4. Brooks, "Self-Awareness May Be Just a Mirage," A23.

religion and Jesus are seen as aids to solving our problems or enhancing our stories. To make it worse, such discussions easily lapse into identifying the problem outside ourselves, in someone else, or some group, thereby assuring ourselves that we are innocent. Through all this Americans assume we have the power to transform ourselves. All that is needed is more confidence or discipline to turn things around. If we gather and only tell our stories and celebrate the values of the status quo—be it a liberal or conservative version—there will be no change.

This prompts the proposal that we need to rethink the role of the sermon in terms of the Word proclaimed which draws forth responses of faith. To initiate such dialogue we will need authentic speech which speaks to the issue of trust of the heart in God. If we are going to ask listeners what they believe, then preachers will have to speak for themselves about what they believe. Such speech will have to be in the face of life in this world where powers conspire against us. Now of course there are more ways to open hearts and encourage a response of faith and love besides the sermon. Scripture, prayers, confession of sin, passing the peace, creeds, testimonies and requests for service also evoke responses.[5] But at this point let us be sure that the sermon opens the dialogue.

This then leads to the second question: the location of the sermon in worship. In most cases it is located in the second half of the service, positioned as the dramatic high point, followed abruptly by the end of the service with a short prayer, final hymn and blessing. This may elevate the sermon but it tends to break the dialectic of Word-response. In effect, appropriate responses to the proclaimed Word are not allowed to happen because the service ends. To be sure, there are human responses earlier in the service, but why are they there and what is their function? What is needed is to re-locate them after the sermon so that congregants are clear on what is happening: We have heard the Word of promise and now it is our time to respond in faith. We cannot keep silent because we are in the process of being changed. The challenge, therefore, is to place after the sermon our response, involving some combination of prayer, credo, passing the peace, the Lord's Prayer, hymns, offering, personal testimonies, confession of sin, Scripture and calls to service. Such a practice might open up the worship in a new way. The Word calls forth faith and we confess faith by these acts.

5. Thomas Lush, a UCC pastor in Pennsylvania, reports how mid-week church dinners have become the means for people to be together after isolation during the pandemic and actually open their hearts and minds in conversation regarding the gospel in the context of scripture and prayer.

3. The Celebration of Joy and Gratitude

Protestant worship has sought to re-create the movement from gathering to remembrance and proclamation, leading to the response of faith, followed by the celebration of joy and gratitude. Such celebration depends on the reality of grace and new life in our midst, which is to say, the presence of Christ and his gifts to us. We do not generate them, nor can we demand them. What we must do in worship is to remember the gifts already bestowed and celebrate the presence of Christ.[6]

Here again we must ask about the current state of the liturgy for services of the Word and the table. One of the frequently offered comments in my life time has been: Why is there so little joy in the celebration of the Lord's Supper? I think the same question could be asked of the service of the Word. My response is that we are still using the medieval framework for the sacrament, which means the service is dominated by the confession of sin, our unworthiness, pleading for mercy and finally a word of forgiveness. Added to this is the fact that when the word of grace is spoken, the service ends with a short prayer, a hymn and blessing. Quite simply, there is no time allocated to the response of faith, joy and gratitude. In the service of the Word, when the sermon is basically the high point the service then ends very quickly.

Let us be clear: I am not proposing that worship be turned into happy talk, with jokes and cute stories or mandatory smiles. There is too much warfare in the world and suffering in our lives. Most people carry disappointment and sorrow, even though they may not mention it. Nor should we forget that the tradition is notable for its insistence that in this life we still struggle with sin and the powers of this world. It is still appropriate to warn against claims to innocence and perfection, or utopian visions of the future. If there is to be joy, it must be based on something new in our lives and the world. The gospel proclaims just such a new reality of God in Christ and the gifts Christ brings. When Luther declared in his famous essay on freedom that the Christian is free, he meant free from the torment of sin and guilt, the obsession with oneself and the acceptance of a new status before God—all in the face of sin, death and the devil. There would be no freedom if the new life in Christ were not actual now. Without the new reality we would still be on the other side of grace, living in the fear of

6. Recall again the powerful image of Calvin's definition of the Lord's Supper: it is like a father, who has already given gifts to the family, now gathers the family again to bestow even more gifts. Cf. *Institutes* IV, ch. XVII, 1359–60.

condemnation and wondering if God is merciful. The point is that we do not begin each day back at the starting point, but live relying on the history of God's grace in our lives.

This suggests that there ought to be a communal celebration of joy and gratitude in our worship. For example, when we confess our sins and receive a word of forgiveness, we must devote time to celebrate that new reality. Passing the peace of Christ calls for a celebration. This is the moment to sing for joy, to confess the faith and offer prayers for the church and world. In other words, the liturgy ought to have time for celebration. The absence of such prompts one to ask whether this is because of our individualistic mindset. Do we assume worship is only directed toward individuals rather than the group, which means communal celebration is not needed? But the primary value of communal worship is to be united together in Christ and discover what it means to participate in a common faith, hope and love. Bear in mind that resistance to sin and the idols of this world must be a communal strategy—a point demonstrated by the Amish. It takes time to generate solidarity within the community and nurture it. Likewise, what differentiates the service of the table from the service of the Word is not that there is *something more* in the bread and wine, but that it is a communal celebration of the presence of Christ and his gifts. This is something we have learned during the years of isolation during the covid pandemic, i.e., the importance of being together! Yet we are treating it like the service is organized for individuals, a theme re-enforced by individuals going forward to receive bread and wine at the table—one at a time! Go back to the basic question: What's happening? If nothing is happening with the community gathered together, then why gather? The sermons could be sent by email. If there is no celebration of the gifts of Christ in the service of the Word or the table, just what is happening?

It is precisely at this point that Black worship offers a positive witness. In the African-American churches, worship is the time for the community to gather apart from a hostile world to affirm their participation in the new life in Christ. It represents a suspension of time, i.e., if time represents the power of the white world to control the hours of the day, in worship one is free from the powers of this world. One can be a human being in a new way and be with the community to praise God, hear the good news and celebrate life together. For this reason, the time of worship is also free: one is not sure when the service will begin or when it will end—a practice frustrating to white people. In this respect, white people miss the point:

if worship is a celebration of freedom with the people of God, why would you want it to end? There is nothing more important. What would have to happen for white worship to gain a sense of that freedom and joy?

Here let us speak of the value of music in our worship. Music awakens the soul, pierces the heart and elevates us to a higher level. It is a sign of what is and what shall be by the glory of God. Just as harmony unites two voices and creates something new which each alone cannot generate, so music points to the reconciliation of God's people in the peace of Christ. When music is joined with words, as in great hymns, it awakens us to the good news and allows us to remember and rejoice. Consider the seventeenth century hymn by Christian Keimann (Keymann) which expresses the heart of evangelical worship. The movement of verses replicates the relation between remembrance/proclamation and the celebration of the reality of new life, as exemplified by joy. To match this grand theme the music is especially spirited. Here are the words to "Oh, Rejoice Ye Christians Loudly."

> 1. Oh, rejoice, ye Christians, loudly, For our joy hath now begun;
> Wondrous things our God hath done. Tell abroad God's goodness proudly,
> Who our race hath honored thus, That God deigns to dwell with us.
> Refrain:
> Joy, O joy, beyond all gladness, Christ has done away with sadness!
> Hence all sorrow and repining, For the Sun of Grace is shining!
> 2. See, my soul, thy Savior chooses Weakness here and poverty;
> In such love he comes to thee Nor the hardest couch refuses;
> All He suffers for thy good To redeem thee by His blood.
> Refrain.
> 3. Lord how shall I thank Thee rightly? I acknowledge that by Thee
> I am saved eternally. Let me not forget it lightly,
> But to Thee at all times cleave And my heart true peace receive.
> Refrain

Here is the call to rejoice based on what God has done in the incarnation of the Word with us. The three verses replicate the classic Protestant movement from call to remembrance, through meditation on the cross to the question of our response. As noted earlier, gratitude is the engine which drives faith, hope and love. How we are to thank God has always been the question leading to praise, confession of sin, the confession of faith, as well as gathering in community, works of love and witness in the world.

As grand as this hymn is, one must recognize that it may not capture the imagination of everyone. For one thing it is clearly expressed in the language of the seventeenth century. Some might wish to see the good news expressed in broader terms than the eternal salvation of the believers. As argued repeatedly, saving power also includes liberation, reconciliation, resistance to the idols, recovery of the true knowledge of God, and especially in our life time, the restoration of the earth. Some might prefer *Amazing Grace*, or *When Peace, Like a River*, or *Lift Every Voice and Sing*, or a hymn of praise by Charles Wesley or even a new hymn. The use of what is called contemporary music reminds us not only of changes in musical style but also different approaches to worship itself. What is crucial is testing hymns by their ability to call to remembrance the grace of God which gathers us into communities of justice and peace.

It also needs to be noted that so much of Protestant hymnody operates out of the piety of gratitude: portraying what God has done and calling believers to rejoice and serve. But even that can be limiting by focusing mostly on the past and/or grace directed toward individuals. By contrast, what emerges from an eschatological perspective is a piety of glory: it looks to the revealing of the reconciliation of all peoples and the restoration of the earth, all embodiments of the glory of God. By directing attention to the present and future, it calls us out of our present comfort zone to participate in the new life being revealed in this world. There is no need to pit the piety of gratitude against the piety of glory, since both reflect the good news in Jesus Christ. Both are needed to point to what God is doing in our lives and in the world. Both are needed to celebrate the good news; both give a basis for celebrations of joy.

In Conclusion

From the beginning it has been argued that centric Protestants are people reformed three times: first by the sixteenth-century Reformation, then by critical issues in the modern world, and in the last century by revolutions in theology and biblical studies in the context of war, genocide and justice for all people. It should not be a surprise to suggest that in light of the past sixty years, the tradition is in need of further reform. The need for change and recovery is obvious. Such efforts will have to claim Luther's conviction that the true treasure of the church is Jesus Christ. And it will also claim that treasure in light of Luther's namesake, Martin Luther King, Jr., who saw in Jesus Christ a new vision for America where all God's people might come together in peace. In other words, it will be about grace and community.

Bibliography

Aulen, Gustaf. *Christus Victor*. Translated by A. G. Hebert. London: SPCK, 1931.

Bernstein, Carl and Robert Woodward. *All the President's Men*. New York: Simon and Shuster, 1974.

Bellah, Robert N. et al. *The Good Society*. New York: Knopf, 1991.

———. *Habits of the Heart: Individualism and Commitment in American Life*. Berkeley: University of California Press, 1985.

Brooks, David. "Self-Awareness May Be Just a Mirage." *New York Times*, September 16, 2021, 23.

Calvin, John. *The Institutes of the Christian Religion*. Translated by Ford Lewis Battles. Edited by John T. McNeill. The Library of Christian Classics, vol. 20. Philadelphia: Westminster, 1960.

Carroll, Jack. *As One With Authority: Reflective Leadership in Ministry*. Louisville: Westminster John Knox, 1991.

Carter, Steven L. *The Culture of Disbelief: How American Law and Politics Trivialize Religious Devotion*. New York: Basic, 1993.

Cone, James. *Black Theology and Black Power*. New York: Seabury, 1969.

Dulles, Avery. *Models of the Church*. New York: Doubleday, 1987.

Eliade, Mircea. *The Myth of the Eternal Return or, Cosmos and History*. Translated by Willard R. Trask. Princeton: Princeton University Press, 1954.

Eliade, Mircea. *The Sacred and the Profane: The Nature of Religion*. Translated by Willard R. Trask. New York: Harper and Row, 1957.

Evans, William B. *Imputation and Impartation: Union with Christ in American Reformed Theology*. Eugene, OR: Wipf and Stock, 2008.

Gutierrez, Gustavo. *Theology of Liberation: History, Politics and Salvation*. Translated and edited by Sister Caridad Inda and John Eagleson. New York: Maryknoll: 1988.

Halberstam, David. *The Best and the Brightest*. New York: Random House, 1972.

Heidelberg Catechism: A New Translation for the 21st Century. Translated by Lee C. Barrett III. Cleveland: Pilgrim, 2007.

Bibliography

Hunter, James Davison. *Culture Wars: The Struggle to Define America.* New York: Basic, 1991.

King, Jr., Martin Luther. "Letter From Birmingham City Jail," Reprinted from *The New Leader*, June 24, 1963.

Luther, Martin. "The Babylonian Captivity of the Church." In *Three Treatises: Martin Luther*, translated by A.T.W. Steinhäuser, 115–261. Philadelphia: Muhlenberg, 1960.

————. "The Blessed Sacrament of the Holy and True Body of Christ, and the Brotherhoods." In *Word and Sacrament* I, edited by E. Theodore Bachmann, 45–73. Luther's Works, vol. 35. Philadelphia: Muhlenberg, 1960.

————. "The Freedom of a Christian." In *Three Treatises: Martin Luther*, translated by W.A. Lambert, 262–316. Philadelphia: Muhlenberg, 1960.

————. *The Large Catechism of Martin Luther.* Translated by Robert H. Fischer. Philadelphia: Fortress, 1960.

————. "Ninety–Five Theses, 1517." Translated by C. M. Jacobs and revised by Harold J. Grimm. In *Career of the Reformer*, edited by Harold J. Grimm, 17–34. Luther's Works, vol. 31. Philadelphia: Muhlenberg, 1957.

————. *Luther: Lectures on Romans.* Edited and Translated by Wilhelm Pauch. The Library of Christian Classics, vol. 15. Philadelphia: Westminster, 1961.

————. "That These Words of Christ, This is My Body, etc., Still Stand Firm Against the Fanatics (1527)." In *Word and Sacrament, III*, edited by Robert H. Fischer, 3–149. Luther's Works, vol. 37. Philadelphia: Muhlenberg, 1961.

————. "Treatise on the New Testament, That is, the Holy Mass." In *Word and Sacrament, I*, edited by E. Theodore Bachmann, 75–112. Luther's Works, vol. 35. Philadelphia: Muhlenberg, 1960.

Millard, Egan. "2019 Parochial reports show continued decline and a 'dire' future for the Episcopal Church." *Episcopal News Service.* https://www.episcopalnewsservice.org/2020/10/16/2019-parochial-reports-show-continued-decline-and-a-dire-future-for-the-episcopal-church/.

Moltmann, Jürgen. *Theology of Hope: On the Ground and Implications of Christian Eschatology.* Translated by James W. Leitch. New York: Harper and Row, 1967.

Niebuhr, H. Richard. "A COMMUNICATION: The Only Way into the Kingdom of God." *The Christian Century*, April 6, 1932, 447.

Niebuhr, Reinhold. *Moral Man and Immoral Society.* New York: Charles Scribner's Sons, 1932.

Oberman, Heiko A. *Luther: Man Between God and the Devil.* Translated by Eileen Walliser-Schwarzbart. New York: Doubleday, 1992.

Ozment, Steven. *The Age of Reform 1250–1550: An Intellectual and Religious History of Late Medieval and Reformation Europe.* New Haven: Yale University Press, 1980.

Roof, Wade Clark and William McKinney. *American Mainline Religion: Its Changing Shape and Future.* New Brunswick: Rutgers University Press, 1987.

Russell, Letty, ed. *Feminist Interpretation of the Bible.* Philadelphia: Westminster, 1985.

Santmire, H. Paul. *The Travail of Nature: The Ambiguous Ecological Promise of Christian Theology.* Philadelphia: Fortress, 1985.

Schaff, Philip. *America: A Sketch of its Political, Social and Religious Character.* Edited by Perry Miller. Cambridge: Belknap, 1961.

————. *The Principle of Protestantism.* Translated by John W. Nevin. Edited by Bard Thompson and George H. Bricker. Philadelphia: United Church Press, 1964.

Bibliography

Schmiechen, Peter. *Christ the Reconciler: A Theology for Opposites, Differences and Enemies*. Grand Rapids: Eerdmans, 1996.

———. *Defining the Church for Our Time: Origin and Structure, Variety and Viability*. Eugene, OR: Wipf and Stock, 2012.

———. *Gift and Promise: An Evangelical Theology of the Lord's Supper*. Eugene, OR: Wipf and Stock, 2017.

———. *Saving Power: Theories of Atonement and Forms of the Church*. Grand Rapids: Eerdmans, 2005.

Schmitt, Pierre. *The Isenheim Altar*. Berne: Hallwag, 1960.

Stendahl, Krister. *Paul Among Jews and Gentiles and Other Essays*. Philadelphia: Fortress, 1976.

Wikipedia. "Evangelical Lutheran Church: History." Last modified April 5, 2022. https://en.wikipedia.org/wiki/Evangelical_Lutheran_Church_in_America#History

Wikipedia. "Irreligion in the US: Demographics." Last modified March 28, 2022. https://en.wikipedia.org/wiki/Irreligion_in_the_United_States#Demographics

Wikipedia. "Lutheran Church—Missouri Synod: Membership and Democraphics." Last modified January 26, 2022. https://en.wikipedia.org/wiki/Lutheran_Church%E2%80%93Missouri_Synod#Membership_and_demographics

Wikipedia. "Presbyterian Church USA: Demographics." Last modified March 17, 2022. https://en.wikipedia.org/wiki/Presbyterian_Church_(USA)#Demographics

Wikipedia. "Southern Baptist: Membership." Last modified April 1, 2022. https://en.wikipedia.org/wiki/Southern_Baptist_Convention#Membership

Wikipedia. "United Church of Christ: Membership." Last modified March 30, 2022. https://en.wikipedia.org/wiki/United_Church_of_Christ#Membership

Wikipedia. "United Methodist Church: Membership Trends." Last modified March 14, 2022. https://en.wikipedia.org/wiki/United_Methodist_Church#Membership_trends